MORE
Happy Quilter
VARIETY PUZZLES

Gailen Runge

60 + Large-Print Word Puzzles
for People Who Love to Sew

VOLUME 3

C&T PUBLISHING

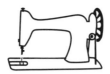

Contents

---

ctpub.com   P.O. Box 1456, Lafayette, CA 94549 | 800.284.1114

Copyright © 2020 by C&T Publishing, Inc. All rights reserved.

PRODUCT TEAM: Gailen Runge, Kerry Graham, Zinnia Heinzmann, and Alice Mace Nakanishi

We take great care to ensure that the information included in our products is accurate and presented in good faith, but no warranty is provided, nor are results guaranteed. Having no control over the choices of materials or procedures used, neither the author nor C&T Publishing, Inc., shall have any liability to any person or entity with respect to any loss or damage caused directly or indirectly by the information contained in this book.

COVER QUILT DETAIL: *Sunrise, Sunset* by Judy Gauthier (from *Sensational Quilts for Scrap Lovers*; C&T Publishing)

Printed in the USA

10 9 8 7 6 5 4 3 2

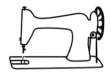

Instructions

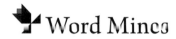 Word Mines

See how many words you can make out of the letters in popular needle styles!

PINS & NEEDLES

B E A D

4-letter words (2)

a b e d

b a d e

3-letter words (4)

b a d

b e d

d a b

d e b

2-letter words (8)

a b

a d

a e

b a

b e

d a

d e

e d

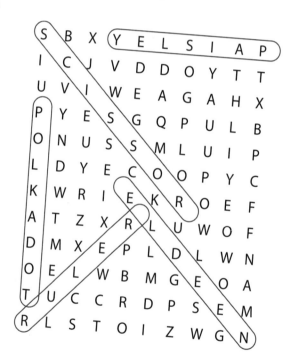 Word RoundUps™

Word RoundUps are a combination of traditional word searches and crossword puzzles. Use the crossword-style clues to identify the hidden words.

Word RoundUp Sample

☑ 3 tools quilters use regularly

☑ 2 fabric patterns that start with **P**

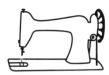

Word Scrambles

Who doesn't love a good word scramble?
Unscramble the letters to find popular quilting terms.

GIDNOI . . . . indigo

RWPOED BULE . . . . powder blue

VYNA . . . . navy

DHMTIIGN . . . . midnight

Criss Crosses

Like Word RoundUps, Criss Cross puzzles are a combination of word searches and crossword puzzles. The grid is like a crossword puzzle, but instead of clues, the words are listed as they are in a word search. Fill the words into their spots in the puzzle, guided by the placement of letters where words cross. *The easiest way to get started is to place words where there is only one option (for example, if there is only one word with three letters). If there aren't any of those, start with a letter grouping with few entries and compare crossing words.*

Quilter Activities

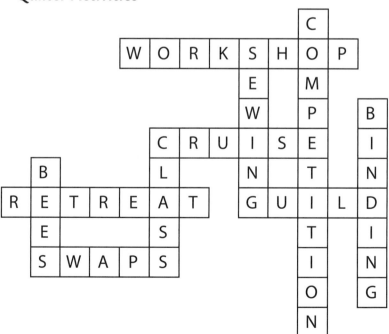

11 letters
COMPETITION

8 letters
WORKSHOP

7 letters
BINDING
RETREAT

6 letters
SEWING
CRUISE

5 letters
GUILD
SWAPS
CLASS

4 letters
BEES

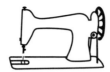

❋ Logic Puzzles

Each logic puzzle is a simple story involving different elements, such as people, places, things, times, and amounts. Your goal in solving a logic puzzle is to figure out the relationship between the different elements. Each logic puzzle has a little background on the story and a list of clues. It's also accompanied by a grid that you can use to help solve the puzzle.

Read through the clues. Each time you learn that two elements are or are not related, record the fact in the grid. If the fact is something that is **not true** (that Sue did not sew the pillow, for example), use an X in the grid. If the fact is **true** (that the fourth speaker sewed the baby quilt), use an O in the grid. Use your deductive reasoning to eliminate options. In clue 1 below, for example, you know that Sue did not sew the anniversary quilt. You also know that the anniversary quilt could not be presented fourth and that Sue could not have spoken first because the anniversary quilt was presented before Sue spoke.

Work through the puzzle in blocks of related facts. When you eliminate all but one possibility for an element in a block, you know that remaining possibility is the correct answer, and you can X out other possibilities for that element. Each positive answer will lead to more related facts, and you will deduce your way to solving the puzzle!

> **June Bug Quilt Meeting**

At the June Bug Quilt Guild's winter meeting, four members showed their new work. Using only the clues that follow, match each member to the item she sewed and the order in which she spoke.

1. The quilter who sewed the anniversary quilt spoke right before Sue.

2. The guild member who spoke second was either Betsy or the quilter who made the wallhanging.

3. The maker of the wallhanging spoke two spots before Alice.

4. Kerry made the anniversary quilt.

5. The last speaker of the evening made the baby quilt.

		QUILTER				PROJECT			
		Betsy	Sue	Kerry	Alice	Wallhanging	Baby quilt	Anniversary quilt	Patchwork pillow
ORDER	1		X		X		X		
	2				X		X		
	3						X		
	4					X	O	X	X
PROJECT	Wallhanging	X		X					
	Baby quilt			X					
	Anniversary quilt	X	X	O	X				
	Patchwork pillow			X					

ORDER	QUILTER	PROJECT
1		
2		
3		
4		Baby quilt

♥ Crossword Puzzles

Solve the clues and enter your answers into the puzzle boxes, following the clue number and word orientation.

❖ Word Searches

Look for the words in the word list in the puzzle. Words can run forward, backward, up, down, and on any diagonal.

Puzzles

♥ Crossword Puzzle 1

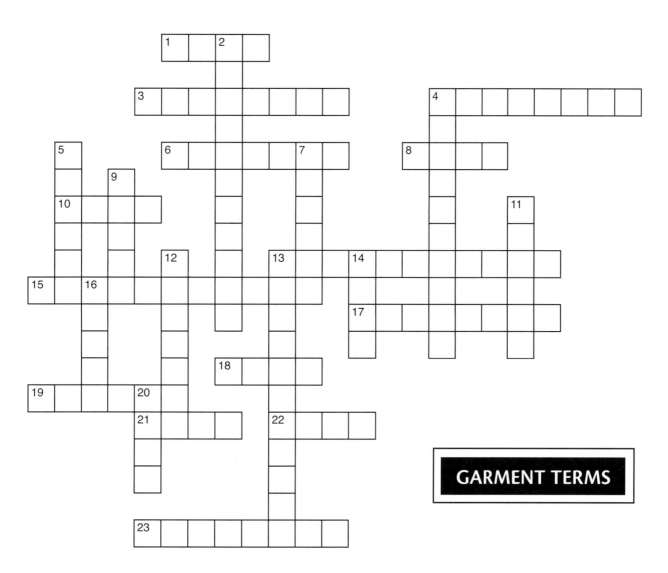

GARMENT TERMS

ACROSS

1   help your convex curves lie flat

3   strong encasing seam (2 wds)

4   many rows of gathers

6   zigzag going nowhere (2 wds)

8   making clear your intentions

10 triangular tuck

13 silky layer to hide it all

15 a warm layer

17 stitched fabric folds

18 don't curse, fix the

19 line ironed in

21 cut away seam allowance

22 stitched fold

23 apparently invisible seam (2 wds)

DOWN

2   a supporting layer

4   stitching inside stitching

5   gets cord through casing

7   tube to hold elastic

9   ability to fall into graceful folds

11 it stiffens and shapes

12 use to pound in creases

13 control for seam allowances

14 distribute fullness

16 be a copycat

20 tape to strengthen a seam

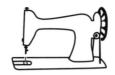

Word Search 1

Color Play

```
P S P R I N G G R E E N T I K A H K R O
Z U F R E B M A V T F Y R E D N E V A L
E Z R W H I T E W B O J T J P K C I R B
N Q C P T L R A B U D M N B C E R P C U
Y M A F L E F M Z B W C A M T U L E A W
F I D N U E A D J B R R L T S E P P I K
L D E R U P T L N L M I P T O I L N P N
W N T J P N K O Z E I M G A N R E O M A
N I B I I E D G H E S G K I D E Y I M
O G L M E A A T M U O O E D D S E D A V
C H U I L E N C L M R N O E L W H R B P
H T E E G A A B H E N G R S K A O C L W
R K C N R L Y T V W I N H C Y O R U U H
E U A A I B U I O D R D A F N V M E S F
X R M L A N L R N A U L D L O G A R M F
O A L B R O B I B R B I T A B L W N N E
```

AMARANTH	CADET BLUE	KHAKI	OLIVE	TEAL
AMBER	CELADON	LAVENDER	ORANGE	TOMATO RED
APPLE	CERISE	LEMON	PEACH	VIOLET
BABY BLUE	CRIMSON	LILAC	PINK	WHITE
BARN RED	EGGPLANT	MAROON	PLUM	WINE
BLACK	EMERALD	MIDNIGHT	PURPLE	
BRICK	FUCHSIA	MINT	RED	
BROWN	GOLD	NAVY	RUST	
BUBBLE GUM	INDIGO	OCHRE	SPRING GREEN	

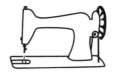

Word Search 2

It's a Matter of Fit

```
M W A I S T G O O F T F A C I N G S K E
S E R B I D Z I O U B E A S E H R Q L M
T E A L I Q B Q B M T B U S T D Q E Y O
Y T S S G C D J B R U S E E W R Z H J L
A N T E U P E N I A A A E J S I P I R S
X E Y S U R O P A Q M A E A S R G P S H
I M L I K E E V S S J P C N M U G T W O
S S I R C Q H M G R Y E O E Y V N A O U
L S N Q A I C N E T T I A C C E R E B L
I E G I B A E J Y N T L A K M V P J L D
N S K J L H V D U A T E S T G O T K E E
E S O F T E O E D S C S S N L R D N X R
K A L G E B P N T I E U I S I H G I H T
Y Z N N C A U R D R J Y Z M M A E S N I
X E K A R O A O S D R Z N N E T R O H S
L D F D F D B A A T P L A C E M E N T I
```

ADJUSTMENTS	BUST	INSEAM	SHORTEN
ARM	CALF	KNEE	SHOULDER
ASSESSMENT	DARTS	LENGTHEN	SIZE
AXIS LINE	DRAPE	MEASUREMENTS	SLOPE
BACK	EASE	NECK	STYLING
BIAS	ELBOW	OUTSEAM	THIGH
BICEP	FACINGS	PLACEMENT	TRIM
BODICE	FOUNDATIONS	RISE	TRYING
BODY TYPE	HIP	SEAMS	WAIST

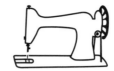

Word Scramble 1

Unscramble the words to find popular quilting terms.

RBA TKCA _ _ _   _ _ _ _

SAGBINT _ _ _ _ _ _ _

TNGCIKA _ _ _ _ _ _ _

IBDNL MHE _ _ _ _ _   _ _ _

GTIRATHS _ _ _ _ _ _ _ _

CETSTRH _ _ _ _ _ _ _

GAZIZG _ _ _ _ _ _

ONHTOBULTE _ _ _ _ _ _ _ _ _ _

HINFNIGIS _ _ _ _ _ _ _ _ _

HCIOCNUG _ _ _ _ _ _ _ _

INRGTGAHE _ _ _ _ _ _ _ _ _

ATNSI _ _ _ _ _

ERLDOL DEEG _ _ _ _ _ _   _ _ _ _

GEDE _ _ _ _

OBLEUD LENEDE _ _ _ _ _ _   _ _ _ _ _ _

ECVTRSCTOHI _ _ _ _ _ _ _ _ _ _ _

CLOAPLS _ _ _ _ _ _ _

ASRCOETV _ _ _ _ _ _ _ _

DEARLD _ _ _ _ _ _

VLOCERKO _ _ _ _ _ _ _ _

DRAOCVTIEE _ _ _ _ _ _ _ _ _ _

OMHCNEBOY _ _ _ _ _ _ _ _ _

ELHLS CKTU _ _ _ _ _ _   _ _ _ _

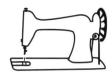

 Word Scramble 2

Unscramble the words to find popular quilting terms.

QUILTING TERMS

EPLISTP _ _ _ _ _ _ _

ROLVALE _ _ _ _ _ _ _

TCKHCBITAS _ _ _ _ _ _ _ _ _

OPOH _ _ _ _

EXSBWAE _ _ _ _ _ _ _

HASTCCRHOS _ _ _ _ _ _ _ _ _ _

NEDGIS _ _ _ _ _ _

HEOC _ _ _ _

DAHN _ _ _ _

ATRFEHE _ _ _ _ _ _ _

ONREFOTIEM _ _ _ _ _ _ _ _ _ _

DEMEANR _ _ _ _ _ _ _

PTOGPAHNRA _ _ _ _ _ _ _ _ _ _

EOSLGV _ _ _ _ _ _

INTGATB _ _ _ _ _ _ _

HTEDRA _ _ _ _ _ _

CITSTH _ _ _ _ _ _

ETI _ _ _

TTOUNPRA _ _ _ _ _ _ _ _

OHTLWELCHO _ _ _ _ _ _ _ _ _ _

IRGD _ _ _ _

TESLINC _ _ _ _ _ _ _

NBSGTIA _ _ _ _ _ _ _

EOSTINN _ _ _ _ _ _ _

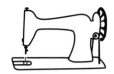

Criss Cross 1

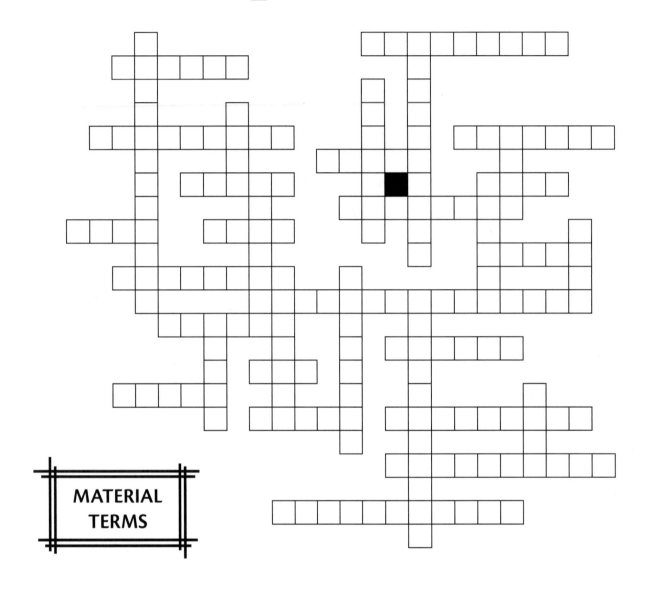

MATERIAL TERMS

15 letters

GARMENT DISTRICT

12 letters

REPRODUCTION

11 letters

DIRECTIONAL

INTERFACING

10 letters

COLLECTION

LENGTHWISE

9 letters

CROSSWISE

STRIKEOFF

8 letters

COLORWAY

DESIGNER

FINISHES

POLYESTER

7 letters

ORGANIC

RIBBING

SELVAGE

YARDAGE

6 letters

MADDER

PRECUT

REPEAT

WEIGHT

5 letters

DRAPE

GRAIN

PRESS

SCRAP

STASH

WEAVE

4 letters

BIAS

BOLT

KNIT

FOLD

PILE

WARP

WEFT

3 letters

NAP

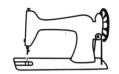

Criss Cross 2

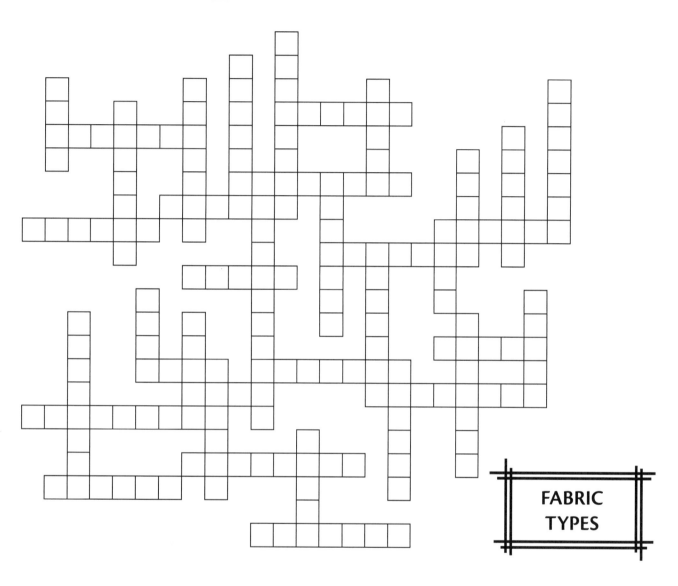

FABRIC TYPES

11 letters

HERRINGBONE

9 letters

POLYESTER

8 letters

CHAMBRAY

CORDUROY

JACQUARD

OILCLOTH

SHANTUNG

7 letters

ACETATE

ACRYLIC

DUCHESS

FLANNEL

GINGHAM

HABUTAI

ORGANIC

ORGANZA

PAISLEY

SPANDEX

TAFFETA

6 letters

CHINTZ

COTTON

EYELET

FLEECE

JERSEY

MUSLIN

VELVET

TARTAN

5 letters

BATIK

LINEN

MINKY

RAYON

SATIN

TWILL

VOILE

4 letters

FELT

KNIT

LAWN

SILK

WOOL

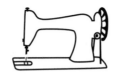

Word RoundUp 1

SEWING SELECTIONS

```
L S O N Y M O V E R L O C K Y I A Q C Q
T X T E M L O H O O P P N Z K K G O Y E
J U P E D O S Q K E G D E E C U T T E L
S W R V A F E E P X J L K H C T E R T S
D C F N R M A O T Z O E S R O S S I C S
E S M L E V E V D N M A T N G T F P J J
Z A E C D D U R G K F U X Y C R V F S P
U B H E N B U A L U B A T V C T A N M T
A E D F I D R N E A X V Z I G Z A G S Y
G E N Q W M Q C D L Q A Z M N V X V V W
E S I O N R U Z I E D W O I V H G N O Q
L W L Q I E O H H X R E Q I S O U O B B
B A B V B G Q Q Z H N E E F C O L N L T
U X X Y B R J Z I O A D D N C Q F F U C
O M F L O E Y Y R Y D L O F E L B U O D
D H M G B S L I K X O M G W E J H O R I
```

☐ ☐ ☐ ☐ ☐ ☐ **6 power tools**

☐ ☐ ☐ ☐ ☐ **5 garment hem options**

☐ ☐ ☐ ☐ **4 hand-quilting helpers**

☐ ☐ ☐ **3 quilt fabrics**

☐ ☐ **2 machine stitches**

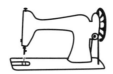

✦ Word RoundUp 2

PROJECT PERFECTION

```
H P Q V I O H M E T B M G I W A S H O E
H E M U V N S O S S C C Y U A S K O O B
C X A K I V O Z X V C Q J L V E S A A K
H C F R V X V T V N P D E G D E V L E S
E U H P J I I T I S T G X G L H T C X N
R C O R N E R S T O N E L V N M U L B N
R R Q W U D V T A J N Z V J U I W L M B
Y I B Z O R H G K W S G V O S H J K T
P M D I W G I Y O Y G N W I O V S S D T
U S E U I K B A Q H I N H Q X D H E A O
E O N E C L V M H D Q S I O F U W A R S
R N W I O P H S N E L N R T B K B L P P
A L R V L H B I S Q S Z W A T S Y U Q U
U B T L E W B H D S H R O P W A R B P N
Q I J L T M W E P O U E O O H R B B U R
S J A D N R B L O C K D S H R D W Q M R
```

☐ ☐ ☐ ☐ ☐ ☐ **6 things on the edge**

☐ ☐ ☐ ☐ ☐ **5 parts of a quilt**

☐ ☐ ☐ ☐ **4 shades of red**

☐ ☐ ☐ **3 fabric preparation terms**

☐ ☐ **2 selections in the fabric store**

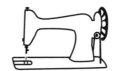

Logic Puzzle 1

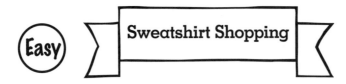

Easy

Sweatshirt Shopping

The Apple Valley Quilt Guild sold several sweatshirts to support its upcoming quilt show. Match each sweatshirt to its buyer, and determine the size and color of each.

1. The extra-large sweatshirt, Toni's shirt, and Bridget's shirt are all different sweatshirts.
2. The red sweatshirt is one size larger than Toni's shirt.
3. Toni's shirt is one size larger than the purple top.
4. Bridget's shirt is larger than Melissa's shirt.
5. Melissa's shirt is one size smaller than the green top.

		BUYER				COLOR			
		Jane	Bridget	Toni	Melissa	Green	Red	Blue	Purple
SIZE	Small								
	Medium								
	Large								
	Extra-large								
COLOR	Green								
	Red								
	Blue								
	Purple								

SIZE	BUYER	COLOR
Small		
Medium		
Large		
Extra-large		

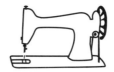

✷ Logic Puzzle 2

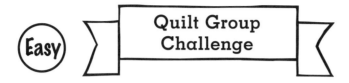

(Easy) > Quilt Group Challenge

There are four quilt projects that each of the members of the Piedmont Pines quilt group challenged themselves to make. Match each quilt to the number of pieces it is made from and who made it first.

1. The Winding Ways quilt was first made by Dina.

2. The Log Cabin quilt has 260 fewer pieces than the quilt first made by Dina.

3. The quilt that has 1,700 pieces was first made by Stacy.

4. The Nine-Patch quilt has 130 fewer pieces than the quilt made by Kris.

		PATTERN				QUILTER			
		Log Cabin	Nine Patch	Winding Ways	Jacob's Ladder	Stacy	Dina	Kris	Jan
PIECES	1,310								
	1,440								
	1,570								
	1,700								
QUILTER	Stacy								
	Dina								
	Kris								
	Jan								

PIECES	PATTERN	QUILTER
1,310		
1,440		
1,570		
1,700		

17

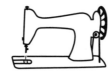

❧ Word Mine 1

See how many words you can make out of the letters in popular needle styles!

PINS & NEEDLES

DENIM

5-letter word (1)

— — — — —

4-letter words (9)

— — — —

— — — —

— — — —

— — — —

— — — —

— — — —

— — — —

— — — —

— — — —

3-letter words (9)

— — —

— — —

— — —

— — —

— — —

— — —

— — —

— — —

— — —

2-letter words (9)

— —

— —

— —

— —

— —

— —

— —

— —

— —

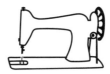

Word Mine 2

See how many words you can make out of the letters in popular needle styles!

5-letter words (2)

— — — — —

— — — — —

4-letter words (12)

— — — —

— — — —

— — — —

— — — —

— — — —

— — — —

— — — —

— — — —

— — — —

— — — —

— — — —

— — — —

3-letter words (16)

— — —

— — —

— — —

— — —

— — —

— — —

— — —

— — —

— — —

— — —

— — —

— — —

— — —

— — —

— — —

— — —

2-letter words (7)

— —

— —

— —

— —

— —

— —

— —

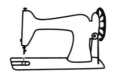

♥ Crossword Puzzle 2

GARMENT PARTS

ACROSS

2 Little Red has one

3 where your arm goes

7 you might stick your thumb through one (2 wds)

10 sleeve with diagonal seam

11 receptacle for keys, wallet, or hands

14 catch a criminal

15 suit structure (2 wds)

16 fabric inserted to create ease

18 fabric that flares out and down

21 what a bird does

22 may be contour, casing, or elastic

23 arms and body are all of one piece (2 wds)

24 what a big bear might do to a little bear acting out

26 upper body section

DOWN

1 top of a dress

4 a slippery layer

5 type of opening

6 part of a round skirt

7 mealtime attire for a toddler

8 you can get grabbed by these

9 a pocket on top

12 Scooby's Velma wore one

13 section inserted for fullness at the hem

14 barely there sleeve

15 can be spaghetti

17 makes the collar stand up

19 tag

20 A-line, pencil, maxi (e.g.)

25 fabric used to finish an unhemmed edge

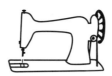

💜 Crossword Puzzle 3

GENERAL SEWING

ACROSS

1 evenly space straight stitch

5 decorative trim

6 fastening with teeth

7 also known as press studs

9 from stitches to edge (2 wds)

13 do this twice before you cut

15 general all-purpose needle

16 change direction around the needle

17 glue with heat

19 incision or division

DOWN

1 frog it or humbling activity

2 bits and pieces to complete things

3 on a 45

4 little spring-loaded scissors

8 a needle pulling thread

10 diagonal join

11 machine that finishes the edges

12 also known as tack

13 leave one's _____

14 decorative fabric add-ons

18 by hand or machine

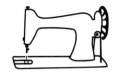

◆ Word Search 3

Quilting Techniques

```
S  T  R  A  V  T  O  E  S  G  E  M  B  E  L  L  I  S  H  U
A  M  O  T  N  U  P  A  R  T  N  O  I  T  A  D  N  U  O  F
T  Y  X  E  O  E  X  J  G  N  I  T  L  I  U  Q  M  H  J  J
I  R  H  G  C  V  M  R  O  K  V  W  A  G  N  I  C  E  I  P
N  X  C  N  D  B  U  Q  Q  Q  N  R  U  T  E  L  D  E  E  N
S  K  T  I  S  E  W  I  N  G  X  Q  E  U  Q  I  L  P  P  A
T  E  I  T  E  A  E  B  I  J  I  C  J  M  G  N  I  S  U  F
I  G  T  T  Q  P  B  U  O  G  U  O  Y  S  A  T  L  I  U  Q
T  N  S  U  G  M  P  D  Y  E  I  N  G  V  E  R  E  Z  L  G
C  I  D  C  N  S  G  Y  X  C  P  I  L  F  D  N  A  W  E  S
H  D  N  Y  I  P  Z  V  S  A  Q  L  A  G  N  I  N  N  I  P
I  A  A  R  H  T  X  L  I  E  N  O  I  T  O  M  E  E  R  F
N  E  P  A  C  N  L  A  Y  A  A  U  G  N  I  S  S  E  R  P
G  B  I  T  T  I  O  B  H  F  R  M  G  N  I  R  E  Y  A  L
Q  W  L  O  O  A  Z  W  S  S  A  L  G  D  E  N  I  A  T  S
G  I  F  R  N  P  G  N  I  N  G  I  S  E  D  G  N  I  Y  T
```

APPLIQUÉ	FUSING	QUILTING
BEADING	LAYERING	ROTARY CUTTING
DESIGNING	NEEDLE-TURN	SATIN STITCHING
DYEING	NOTCHING	SEW AND FLIP
EMBELLISH	PAINT	SEWING
EPP	PIECING	STAINED GLASS
FLIP AND STITCH	PINNING	TRAPUNTO
FOUNDATION	PRESSING	TYING
FREE-MOTION	QUILT-AS-YOU-GO	Y-SEAM

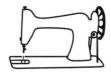

Word Search 4

Sewing Machine Parts

```
S C R E W S S D R P V T H R E A D E R Z
K P D N B C N U S C V A K F L A U N A M
P N R E K O O L Y H R M E T X B Q J W B
N Z I I Z N B R S J U E E T A L P D H Z
P R Z F N S E B D H T T F H V P X F P O
A Q K R E G S E I N A B T G O D D E E F
C C T H Y B Z N L N Z N R L B T V K V L
L A J L K Z J R U I Q X K E E F V B L T
O W F H A B H E W L F F L C Q H L C A W
O P E D A L C V E V O T T V X U O B V I
P M N L M T T O R Z R O R A B E L O C N
S E H L F S I C C E K M P T T E V U K D
E E M A R H W E S H Y H H E E B O N K E
S O H A M B S C T R K G T A R M M O Z R
A S E G E K W A E A I P X G S V E J D J
C G N M O T O R S L K U Z Q Z A F R M C
```

BELT	KNOB	SHAFT
BOBBIN	LIGHT BULB	SHANK
CASE	LOOPER	SHUTTLE HOOK
CORD	MANUAL	SPOOL CAP
FEED DOG	MOTOR	SPRING
FEET	PEDAL	SWITCH
FLY	PLATE	TABLE
GEARS	RACE COVER	THREADER
KNEE-LIFT	SCREWS	WINDER
KNIFE	SET SCREW	

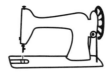

Word Scramble 3

Unscramble the words to find popular quilting terms.

EMIHBLT _ _ _ _ _ _ _

NBGIKCLO _ _ _ _ _ _ _ _

IHSCTT _ _ _ _ _ _

HNCOICGU _ _ _ _ _ _ _ _

DOUCTNE _ _ _ _ _ _ _

HNASCCHSRGOTI _ _ _ _ _ _ _ _ _ _ _ _ _

RNAD _ _ _ _

ROMERYDIBE _ _ _ _ _ _ _ _ _

VANEEEWEV _ _ _ _ _ _ _ _ _

INCWKLENACIDG _ _ _ _ _ _ _ _ _ _ _ _

EEY _ _ _

SSOLF _ _ _ _ _

OHOP _ _ _ _

CAIETNHELA _ _ _ _ _ _ _ _ _ _

NEESLDE _ _ _ _ _ _ _

WNLOEDEREK _ _ _ _ _ _ _ _ _ _

EPLER OCNOTT _ _ _ _ _   _ _ _ _ _ _

RDRWEOK _ _ _ _ _ _ _

MAESRLP _ _ _ _ _ _ _

ESW _ _ _

AREDHT _ _ _ _ _ _

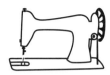

Word Scramble 4

Unscramble the words to find popular quilting terms.

EDINABG   _ _ _ _ _ _ _

LSNOMDNIAIE   _ _ _ _ _ _ _ _ _ _

NSHBIILEMELG   _ _ _ _ _ _ _ _ _ _ _

EHPDT   _ _ _ _ _

DXEMI AMIED   _ _ _ _ _   _ _ _ _ _

CEUSARF GDSIEN   _ _ _ _ _ _ _   _ _ _ _ _ _

AIPNT   _ _ _ _ _

RAHEDT CSGEITKHN   _ _ _ _ _ _   _ _ _ _ _ _ _ _ _

AECLLOG   _ _ _ _ _ _ _

IAEGLNYR   _ _ _ _ _ _ _ _

DYENGI   _ _ _ _ _ _

RIACBF FNDGIOL   _ _ _ _ _ _   _ _ _ _ _ _ _

OVAIMIROTNPSI   _ _ _ _ _ _ _ _ _ _ _ _ _

KIN   _ _ _

NLAADESPC   _ _ _ _ _ _ _ _ _

OTPOH EFRATSRN   _ _ _ _ _   _ _ _ _ _ _ _ _

SIRBHOI   _ _ _ _ _ _ _

ART QUILTING

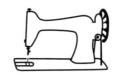

Criss Cross 3

QUILT PARTS

17 letters

DOUBLE-FOLD BINDING

13 letters

PRAIRIE POINTS

12 letters

BUTTED BORDER

MITRED BORDER

11 letters

BIAS BINDING

CORNERSTONE

10 letters

FOUNDATION

8 letters

APPLIQUÉ

QUILTING

SANDWICH

7 letters

BACKING

BASTING

BATTING

BINDING

SASHING

6 letters

BORDER

LAYERS

PIPING

SETTING

SLEEVE

STITCH

5 letters

BLOCK

LABEL

PATCH

PIECE

4 letters

SEAM

TAPE

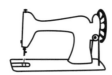

Criss Cross 4

10 letters	5 letters	4 letters
CHAIN	ALIGN	FOLD
PIECE	BASTE	FUSE
7 letters	BLOCK	IRON
MEASURE	COUCH	MARK
PREWASH	MATCH	SNIP
6 letters	MITER	TRIM
CENTER	PRESS	**3 letters**
CREASE	QUILT	CUT
DESIGN	UNSEW	RIP
LAYER		TIE
STITCH		SEW

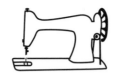

Word RoundUp 3

SEWING SUPERSTARS

```
S F K L I M E T A S B Q R H A D R I H H
N T T E H W A K S N A P K O I P L O O T
I D I N D W A D X D Y S P O Q P M O H U
P N V T Z N P H D E A W Z K X D K R E E
Z A A E C F S Q Y E E E I A L A E S O M
I H M Y D H J O K Y R S I N N A D Z O I
P E B E L B I F C H J N Z D D F Y A J T
P H U C I A H N B Q I N E L J K S P Y N
E T T F F K R W T P G Y R O S C R Y F I
R N T K I C L V T H E O Z O D E K P F H
P I O E R O L K E X E T K P I L C Q X C
F D N S U A K E S L B D D W U R J A N T
X R E I A T U H N I W B I S S Y E H L I
C I B A K S U H T V P W R T M U T P Y T
T B D M H T R O C U I M H C L K Z U S
I N D I G O O X H X C P R E T H H O D S
```

☐ ☐ ☐ ☐ ☐ ☐ **6 closures**

☐ ☐ ☐ ☐ ☐ **5 sewing actions**

☐ ☐ ☐ ☐ **4 thread companies**

☐ ☐ ☐ **3 sewing-related phrases**

☐ ☐ **2 traditional natural dyes**

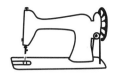

Word RoundUp 4

PIECING PROFESSION

```
V P F E A T H E R S D O X V J N N J M L
S D Z T D E G R E S D L O F E L B U O D
T S M R O J O H M K A W D N U O B J O O
R Q I I J V G N I D N I B T E K N A L B
A Y U N F Q M D W H U Q L F Q B M L J A
I E S I G R L A P P E D V I O Q B C G P
G N W Y L L H P L M C C A L L S G T I F
H R Y T R T E M B Q Y F V R U R M L L Q
T N E I E T S F U L H M N W P R L A X N
L E P C B C B T O M P P U P E O T B G P
I L A I H N E Q P L J W E V W F Y L V S
N P T L O R G I X X D W O C E X Z W K G
E P S P D H I C P S I D A L V V Y S H X
V I A M B Y J V G J L S L C Z Z R V E F
H T I I L A Y E R O E E L G H C N E R F
W S B S X J K O F A N U I R E D N A E M
```

6 binding terms

5 garment seam treatments

4 quilting patterns

3 quilt construction steps

2 pattern companies

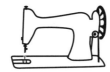

✳ Logic Puzzle 3

A little challenging

Quilting Queries

Four quilters went into Cotton Patch, their local quilt store, for some advice. Match the quilter with the time he or she visited the shop and the challenge to discuss.

1. The quilter needing help with mitered bindings went into the shop an hour before Linda.

2. The four quilters who went into the shop are the person who arrived at 11 a.m., Alice, the person who needs batting, and the quilter struggling with bindings.

3. The quilter who arrived at 11 a.m. is either the person excited to try curved piecing or the one shopping for batting.

4. The quilter trying curved piecing visited Cotton Patch sometime before Sarah.

5. Of the quilter who arrived at 1 p.m. and the one who wanted some advice on curved piecing, one is Linda and the other is Alice.

		QUILTER				CHALLENGE			
		ALICE	TIM	LINDA	SARAH	CUT-OFF CORNERS	CURVED PIECING	MITERING BINDINGS	SELECTING BATTING
TIME	10 a.m.								
	11 a.m.								
	12 noon								
	1 p.m.								
CHALLENGE	Cut-off corners								
	Curved piecing								
	Mitering bindings								
	Selecting batting								

TIME	QUILTER	CHALLENGE
10 a.m.		
11 a.m.		
12 noon		
1 p.m.		

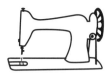

✺ Logic Puzzle 4

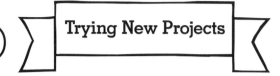

A little challenging

Trying New Projects

Four sewists took classes to try out a new project to use their favorite fabric designer's new release. Determine the month each sewist took a class, what project she wanted to try, and the pattern of the fabric she loves.

1. The plaid fabric was used in a class one month after the bike basket was made.

2. The project started in April was either the tunic or Betsy's project.

3. The floral fabric was either turned into shorts or the place mats.

4. Jennifer's favorite designer's new fabric release was floral.

5. Of the class taken in February and the gingham fabric, one involved place mats and one was chosen by Zinnia.

6. Zinnia's class wasn't in January.

7. The plaid fabric was not used in the tunic or in the place mats.

		SEWIST				PROJECT				FABRIC PATTERN			
		Zinnia	Jennifer	Amber	Betsy	Tunic	Shorts	Bike basket	Place mat	Gingham	Paisley	Floral	Plaid
MONTH	January												
	February												
	March												
	April												
FABRIC PATTERN	Gingham												
	Paisley												
	Floral												
	Plaid												
PROJECT	Tunic												
	Shorts												
	Bike basket												
	Place mat												

MONTH	SEWIST	PROJECT	PATTERN
January			
February			
March			
April			

31

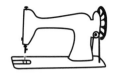

❧ Word Mine 3

See how many words you can make out of the letters in popular needle styles!

PINS & NEEDLES

CREWEL

5-letter word (1)

— — — — —

4-letter words (9)

— — — —

— — — —

— — — —

— — — —

— — — —

— — — —

— — — —

— — — —

3-letter words (10)

— — —

— — —

— — —

— — —

— — —

— — —

— — —

— — —

— — —

— — —

2-letter words (5)

— —

— —

— —

— —

— —

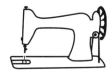

❧ Word Mine 4

See how many words you can make out of the letters in popular needle styles!

PINS & NEEDLES

S H A R P

5-letter word (1)

— — — — —

4-letter words (9)

— — — —

— — — —

— — — —

— — — —

— — — —

— — — —

— — — —

— — — —

— — — —

3-letter words (15)

— — —

— — —

— — —

— — —

— — —

— — —

— — —

— — —

— — —

— — —

— — —

— — —

— — —

— — —

— — —

2-letter words (6)

— —

— —

— —

— —

— —

— —

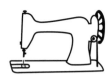

♥ Crossword Puzzle 4

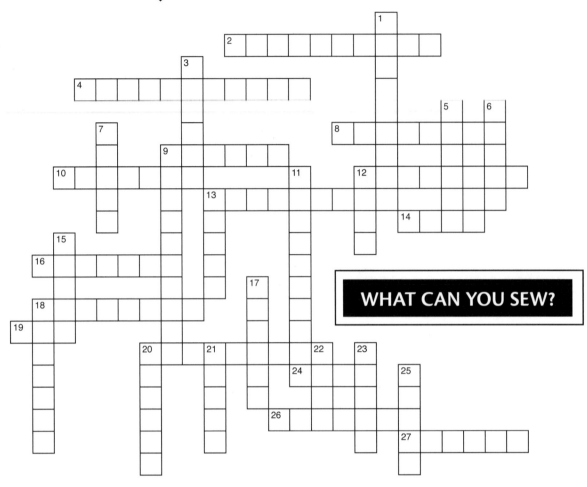

WHAT CAN YOU SEW?

ACROSS

2 cover for a dining surface

4 fabric art

8 alternative to dog-ears

9 a place to lay your head

10 bangs style

12 might be part of a sheet set (2 wds)

13 protection for a sofa (2 wds)

14 type of bag

16 quilt and pillow in one

18 piece of table decor

19 boater, deerstalker (i.e.)

20 quilt or coverlet (e.g.)

24 long, loose outer garment

26 dust ruffle

27 shirks work (_____ off)

DOWN

1 might replace a jacket (2 wds)

3 serviette

5 English baked potato

6 kind of steak

7 __ one's lips

9 cushion cover (2 wds)

11 workout clothes (2 wds)

12 __ it out

13 eat greedily

15 can be wholecloth, patchwork, or appliqué

17 coffee cup mat (2 wds)

18 sleepover wear

20 a member of the Portland basketball team

21 style of dress or jacket

22 diminutive name for a sweetheart

23 invented by Levi Strauss

25 you can do it up or down

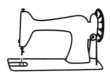

♥ Crossword Puzzle 5

ACROSS

3 material for a killer pair of pants

7 advanced DIY home decor project

8 high notes

11 grab (up)

12 top part of the body

13 thread art that can be woven or embroidered

17 species of dragonfly

19 needles for threading thick yarns

22 long, colorful pin

24 thread's target

26 lend a helping ___

27 hat maker

28 needle good for cross-stitch (2 wds)

DOWN

1 type of pen

2 has eye and comes to a point

4 straight pin for sewing

5 key feature of a vinyl record

6 part of a spear

9 the apex is a high one

10 used for threading elastic

11 post-workout activity

13 finger protector

14 part of this puzzle's theme

15 leg between the knee and ankle

16 ___ Studios Hollywood

18 needlework

20 tufted velvety yarn

21 hand quilting needles are called

23 popular jacket fabric

25 Singer (i.e.)

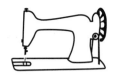

✦ Word Search 5

Design Tools

```
V  R  E  Q  C  A  L  C  U  L  A  T  O  R  R  D  E  Y  N  V
C  O  M  P  U  T  E  R  H  J  I  B  D  K  J  U  O  I  E  R
W  I  N  S  T  A  G  R  A  M  Q  N  A  S  D  D  D  L  J  M
R  N  V  M  M  D  E  B  J  K  L  L  T  V  H  E  L  P  X  O
U  S  X  Z  A  P  Y  J  R  C  P  W  W  U  A  U  U  G  L  C
L  P  R  O  Z  A  J  N  X  X  H  T  G  S  M  S  T  X  R  Z
E  I  Q  R  T  P  L  A  R  F  C  R  S  B  A  S  K  E  L  P
R  R  Y  G  S  E  W  L  V  Z  P  L  E  E  R  O  A  O  A  R
O  A  X  P  S  R  N  P  A  E  A  T  E  H  R  T  S  T  O  A
X  T  V  R  A  M  L  S  N  W  A  F  S  T  I  E  T  X  R  B
R  I  E  G  L  I  X  S  L  L  N  R  E  V  R  E  T  R  O  R
M  O  N  I  C  A  L  L  O  I  H  G  I  E  R  C  E  N  W  Y
U  N  U  O  Q  W  H  C  I  R  C  T  I  N  I  S  I  L  I  U
H  R  L  R  Y  D  O  A  J  S  Y  N  U  S  A  L  Q  S  V  P
H  G  R  A  P  H  P  A  P  E  R  O  E  R  E  R  D  R  U  E
R  E  B  B  C  N  T  E  B  V  R  D  E  P  R  D  K  H  A  M
```

BOOKS	ERASER	PATTERN
CALCULATOR	GRAPH PAPER	PENCILS
CHOCOLATE	IDEAS	PENS
CLASS	INSPIRATION	PINTEREST
COMPUTER	INSTAGRAM	PLAN
CREATIVITY	MUSIC	RULER
DESIGN WALL	PAPER	VELLUM

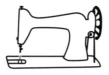

Word Search 6

Interfacing

```
A N D Z U O R N T A N C L N E F F I T S
Q L T S W A I T K V O M O J T N E V O W
D F F L P K L K C V X G A N K N Y Z X Y
L U E E X E Y U E A U W C R H D I G I R
A S A E D X R R E E Y G H N F W C F
J I T S V J A M C P Q D T V O C P E E U
D B H G T G C E A Z A H Y N S U U Q S S
Q L E H E A E M J N G T W W D T P B A I
D E R O T L B O C I E O E E G T R L H B
C T W W F G L I E K V N T R R F K D X L
E A E I D A N W L E D A T X U E E T W E
D P I U Z M Y E N I L H T X F S V S N A
E E G A V V P J R U T F U R T M S C Q M
M C H G A A R N S T A Y H H I V B E J M
O U T E H C R N T R S U V X N C C E R K
H H H S V J I Q C A P P S W K T Q O W P
```

BUCKRAM

COVERAGE

CRAFT

FEATHERWEIGHT

FLEECE

FUSIBLE

FUSIBLE TAPE

HEAVYWEIGHT

HOME DEC

INSULATED

KNIT

NONWOVEN

PERMANENT

PRESSURE TAPE

RIGID

SEWIN

SHAPE

STABILITY

STIFFEN

STRENGTH

WEB

WOVEN

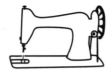

⊞ Word Scramble 5

Unscramble the words to find popular quilting terms.

CLEANED AND
PRESSED

RINO _ _ _ _

EAMST _ _ _ _ _

ESRPS TCOLH _ _ _ _ _ _ _ _ _ _

SMEA LRLO _ _ _ _ _ _ _ _

AHM _ _ _

VEESLE ORADB _ _ _ _ _ _ _ _ _ _ _

SELO EAPTL _ _ _ _ _ _ _ _ _

GNHA UTO _ _ _ _ _ _ _

ULNERDA _ _ _ _ _ _ _

LBDEE _ _ _ _ _

URN _ _ _

RPNTEANEM PESSR _ _ _ _ _ _ _ _ _ _ _ _ _ _

PRDI YRD _ _ _ _ _ _ _

ALUDRNE _ _ _ _ _ _ _

NSIP _ _ _ _

ODAL _ _ _ _

WAHS _ _ _ _

ECBALH _ _ _ _ _ _

ANHG _ _ _ _

NDAH WAHS _ _ _ _ _ _ _ _

EETALCID _ _ _ _ _ _ _ _

RACE _ _ _ _

INFSHI _ _ _ _ _ _

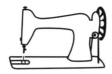

Word Scramble 6

Unscramble the words to find popular quilting terms.

COLOR WHEEL

OOUNSAGLA _ _ _ _ _ _ _ _ _

OCLRO TOREYH _ _ _ _ _   _ _ _ _ _ _

INTT _ _ _ _

VAUEL _ _ _ _ _

CRLOO HWELE _ _ _ _ _   _ _ _ _ _

LOOC _ _ _ _

EYD _ _ _

RAYG SAELC _ _ _ _   _ _ _ _ _

EUH _ _ _

SHEAD _ _ _ _ _

ERNMMALCTYOPE _ _ _ _ _ _ _ _ _ _ _ _ _

CRIIDTA _ _ _ _ _ _ _

NLNEGBDI _ _ _ _ _ _ _ _

LUAEV ERDIFN _ _ _ _ _   _ _ _ _ _ _

MRAW _ _ _ _

ATONRTSAIU _ _ _ _ _ _ _ _ _ _

RYMIRAP _ _ _ _ _ _ _

RADENYOSC _ _ _ _ _ _ _ _ _

REIAYRTT _ _ _ _ _ _ _ _

NTEO _ _ _ _

UMPCRSET _ _ _ _ _ _ _ _

39

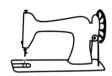

QUILT STYLES

Criss Cross 5

15 letters

MARINERS COMPASS

12 letters

POSTAGE STAMP

STAINED GLASS

11 letters

FRENCH BRAID

HISTORICAL

TRADITIONAL

10 letters

WHOLECLOTH

INNOVATIVE

9 letters

GEOMETRIC

LANDSCAPE

MEDALLION

MINIATURE

PICTORIAL

8 letters

APPLIQUÉ

ART QUILT

BARGELLO

DEAR JANE

ONE BLOCK

7 letters

ANTIQUE

SAMPLER

SCRAPPY

VINTAGE

6 letters

MODERN

STRING

T-SHIRT

5 letters

AMISH

CRAZY

CHARM

STORY

STRIP

4 letters

TIED

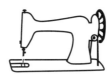

Criss Cross 6

13 letters

SCISSOR KEEPER

SEWING MACHINE

12 letters

COLOR PENCILS

FREEZER PAPER

10 letters

GRAPH PAPER

PINCUSHION

9 letters

CHOCOLATE

SAFETY PIN

SEAM GUIDE

STEAMLESS

8 letters

BETWEENS

SCISSORS

STILETTO

TEMPLATE

7 letters

BATTING

BEESWAX

LONGARM

STEAMER

STENCIL

THIMBLE

6 letters

BOBBIN

CAMERA

ERASER

NEEDLE

STARCH

THREAD

VELLUM

ZIPPER

5 letters

CHALK

RULER

SNIPS

4 letters

ETUI

FEET

HOOP

IRON

PINS

TAPE

3 letters

OIL

PIN

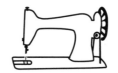

Word RoundUp 5

PLAYING WITH NOTIONS

```
P  I  J  Q  O  S  H  B  C  A  X  E  V  E  E  L  S  N  I  P
C  I  N  E  E  D  L  E  H  I  M  O  V  E  D  A  S  K  W  F
C  H  P  Z  Z  K  X  T  A  H  L  I  I  E  S  Q  K  D  O  H
Z  Z  V  I  G  T  L  K  L  T  I  O  E  O  T  Q  G  R  J  C
X  L  C  A  N  P  A  Z  K  S  N  T  E  Y  J  Q  R  Q  H  W
H  E  W  O  X  G  B  A  M  W  I  M  Z  V  X  E  Y  W  O  L
M  T  B  N  L  G  E  M  A  X  N  H  L  J  S  X  N  N  M  H
D  C  F  D  C  L  L  P  R  N  G  Q  M  T  W  O  D  O  A  N
X  W  Q  T  A  J  A  P  K  W  Z  Z  X  D  S  I  E  T  L  O  H
A  I  Z  A  H  P  S  R  E  I  F  M  X  H  R  K  D  E  U  H
W  Z  P  T  G  S  D  D  R  W  T  I  S  C  U  T  N  N  P  E
S  U  E  Y  E  K  I  H  M  Z  Q  U  L  K  G  N  E  E  K  H
E  V  O  L  T  K  Q  H  G  Y  C  I  V  I  G  P  B  H  K  D
E  S  O  N  P  Z  C  Y  V  N  P  B  T  G  N  I  D  N  I  B
B  B  I  Z  E  P  Q  O  I  S  P  M  D  D  L  A  R  E  M  E
J  M  P  Q  J  V  A  P  P  A  J  E  D  A  H  S  F  F  U  C
```

☐ ☐ ☐ ☐ ☐ ☐ **6 notions**

☐ ☐ ☐ ☐ ☐ **5 parts to sewing a jacket**

☐ ☐ ☐ **3 green varieties**

☐ ☐ ☐ **3 quilt finishing touches**

☐ ☐ **2 color terms**

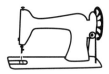

Word RoundUp 6

FABRIC FUN

```
J S M C O N V E R S A T I O N D B I X W
R K H J J D Q C F Z W Z J G N I K I V S
O R J E R E Z T L Z J W S Q R H W R N O
T V M Z A S P I R T S E O T T E L I T S
A G M X Y R J F E S A T F C E U H G E H
R O B E E S N E M Y H C F W P P D K E
Y J G E C L O R M L L I W R G S O W R
C W J T Y B G I G D M N D R E H T O R B
U J V R I N P E E A K E Q U R E G N I S
T M A R A P O J L Y R S R O S S I C S J
T E C I E O P A T E E J B G E J F L W I
E H R R V F R I K G L D V B N Q Q D E V
R T B Q I O L C B E R N I N A I X N D L
O M T Y L I E W D L Z U T O D A K L O P
J R L F T H E L O O A S D S E R A U Q S
R A Y U C L H C Y M Y D Q E D A C O R B
```

☐ ☐ ☐ ☐ ☐ ☐   **6 sharp tools**

☐ ☐ ☐ ☐ ☐   **5 fabric prints**

☐ ☐ ☐ ☐   **4 sewing machine brands**

☐ ☐ ☐   **3 shapes of precuts**

☐ ☐   **2 quilt sizes**

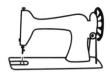

✳ Logic Puzzle 5

Flower Embroidery

Four members of the garden club are also excellent embroiderers. They decided to embroider their favorite flower onto small projects to sell at the garden-club fundraiser. Match each person with their favorite flower, the project they embroidered, and how much they charged for their creations.

1. The needle artist who sold sachets doesn't love irises.

2. Between Dawn and the embroiderer who loves peonies, one sold hooped wall art and the other sold sachets.

3. Of the embroiderer who charged $3 for her creations and the one who loves violets, one sold sachets and the other was Amy.

4. The flower lover who made cuff bracelets charged more than the embroiderer who loves irises.

5. Amy sold cuff bracelets.

6. The embroiderer who loves peonies charged $4 more than Lynn.

		EMBROIDERER				FLOWER				PROJECT			
		Jessica	Lynn	Dawn	Amy	Rose	Violet	Peony	Iris	Hooped wall art	Gift tags	Cuff bracelet	Sachet
PRICE	$3												
	$5												
	$7												
	$9												
PROJECT	Hooped wall art												
	Gift tags												
	Cuff bracelet												
	Sachet												
FLOWER	Rose												
	Violet												
	Peony												
	Iris												

PRICE	EMBROIDERER	FLOWER	PROJECT
$3			
$5			
$7			
$9			

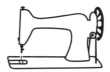

✳ Logic Puzzle 6

Intermediate ⟩ **Road Trips!** ⟨

A group of friends who are spread across the States love to get together for an annual quilt retreat. Each year one of the friends organizes the trip for her home state and sets a challenge theme. Determine each trip's host, quilting theme, state, and year the trip occurred.

1. The Ohio quilt retreat either had an appliqué theme or the trip was planned by Roxane.

2. The trip planned by Roxane was not in 2017.

3. The retreat planned by Liz was either rainbow-themed or the trip to Kentucky.

4. The four quilt retreats were Ohio holiday, the rainbow-themed challenge, and the trips in 2018 and 2019.

5. Of the holiday organized by Liz and the traditional-quilt challenge, one was in 2018 and the other was in Kentucky.

6. Of the trip with the traditional-quilt theme and the trip to Indiana, one was arranged by Tristan and the other was in 2016.

		FRIEND				THEME				STATE			
		Debbie	Liz	Roxane	Tristan	Rainbow	Appliqué	Stash busting	Traditional	Ohio	Kentucky	Indiana	Illinois
YEAR	2016												
	2017												
	2018												
	2019												
STATE	Ohio												
	Kentucky												
	Indiana												
	Illinois												
THEME	Rainbow												
	Appliqué												
	Stash busting												
	Traditional												

YEAR	FRIEND	THEME	STATE
2016			
2017			
2018			
2019			

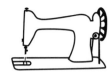

Word Mine 5

See how many words you can make out of the letters in popular needle styles!

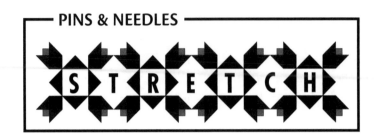

PINS & NEEDLES

STRETCH

6-letter word (1)	4-letter words (21)	3-letter words (17)	2-letter words (8)
_ _ _ _ _ _	_ _ _ _	_ _ _	_ _
	_ _ _ _	_ _ _	_ _
5-letter words (8)	_ _ _ _	_ _ _	_ _
	_ _ _ _	_ _ _	_ _
_ _ _ _ _	_ _ _ _	_ _ _	_ _
_ _ _ _ _	_ _ _ _	_ _ _	_ _
_ _ _ _ _	_ _ _ _	_ _ _	_ _
_ _ _ _ _	_ _ _ _	_ _ _	_ _
_ _ _ _ _	_ _ _ _	_ _ _	
_ _ _ _ _	_ _ _ _	_ _ _	
_ _ _ _ _	_ _ _ _	_ _ _	
_ _ _ _ _	_ _ _ _	_ _ _	
	_ _ _ _	_ _ _	
	_ _ _ _	_ _ _	
	_ _ _	_ _ _	
	_ _ _	_ _ _	
	_ _ _	_ _ _	
	_ _ _		
	_ _ _		
	_ _ _		
	_ _ _		

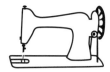

★ Word Mine 6

See how many words you can make out of the letters in popular needle styles!

PINS & NEEDLES

DARNER

6-letter word (1)

— — — — — —

5-letter words (6)

— — — — —

— — — — —

— — — — —

— — — — —

— — — — —

— — — — —

4-letter words (13)

— — — —

— — — —

— — — —

— — — —

— — — —

— — — —

— — — —

— — — —

— — — —

— — — —

— — — —

— — — —

— — — —

3-letter words (14)

— — —

— — —

— — —

— — —

— — —

— — —

— — —

— — —

— — —

— — —

— — —

— — —

— — —

— — —

2-letter words (12)

— —

— —

— —

— —

— —

— —

— —

— —

— —

— —

— —

— —

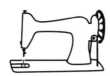

♥ Crossword Puzzle 6

ACROSS

5 cloth

6 related to the home

7 circular blade (2 wds)

8 postpone

10 mannequin (2 wds)

12 ideas

14 type of ship

16 rubbish receptacle (2 wds)

17 queen of all she surveys

18 padded flat surface (2 wds)

20 sharp shapers

21 table top protector (2 wds)

23 Something the sun provides

26 spindle (2 wds)

27 sewing room tomato (2 wds)

DOWN

1 what a closet provides

2 serger's stitch

3 project instructions

4 zigzag cutters (2 wds)

9 embellishment

11 overlock machine

13 material inventory

15 light-bulb moment

18 one-stop shop for seams

19 a place to play with your art (2 wds)

22 _____ of the law

24 fine filament

25 head of a board of directors

26 ____ a hotel room

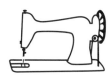

Crossword Puzzle 7

FABRIC PATTERNS

ACROSS

3 with small elements scattered across it

5 colors taking turns

8 circle, square, rectangle elements

9 buta

10 print to talk about?

11 it was so good then let's do it again!

16 shape of a V

17 great for quilt backs

19 the inside structure of a fish?

20 Baltimore Album motif

22 found on a fancy couch

23 you have to earn these

DOWN

1 tartan tweed

2 more than one of the same

3 Amy Butler, Tula Pink, Cotton + Steel (i.e.)

4 a measure of maturity

6 more than 100 years old

7 cats and cottons

12 the big picture

13 from one to another

14 good for "I spy" quilts

15 woven weave

18 a dance of spots? (2 wds)

19 a character in traditional pantomime

21 tone on tone with a sheen

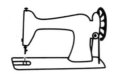

Word Search 7

General Sewing

```
D E P M Q Z M U W O L L I U Q W Z B L C
A P W M U F A B R I C S T O R E V P I Z
R E M M U D M V B I E N I A L E T A H C
N F S U N S I L G Z E V S Q S N I P G N
S J A U O I L N X E Q N S U T Q N C N A
Y E C S F E I I D L O P G Y A E T C I O
C Z A T T P Y L N I O K K M T P E E R G
Q T K M I E E Q T O N V A U S L R E R N
T S O P S S N O L I U E I I T Z F M I I
N E G N T T N E E S S H S T S A O H H
I H Z H V C R E R H P X V S F T C H S C
K C E E C H S E C S V C D W P A I J L U
D E Q V S A C N S I P I N S S S N X Y R
O P K C E S E T I S R Y A V E H G F C M
B O M R I R Y K A R E H S A D R E B A H
A H C S F V P M T P R E K A M S S E R D
```

BODKIN	HABERDASHER	PIPING
CHATELAINE	HOME EC	QUILLOW
CREASE	HOPE CHEST	RUCHING
DARN	INTERFACING	SEAMSTRESS
DRESS MAKER	MUSLIN	SHIRRING
ETUI	NEEDLES	SNIP
FABRIC STORE	NOTIONS	SPOOL
FASTENERS	PATCH	STASH
FRENCH SEAM	PINS	ZIP
FUSE		

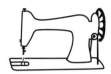

Word Search 8

Quilter's Activities

```
P H M W V V B B Y P O H S K R O W K V O
S I J S G N I T C E L L O C C I R B A F
L R N R E U M N V M X F L U E S I U R C
I X G T E W S G W F C W F L W D M T S G
C L P P E T I B U Q V S O A G I C L H N
E S G K S R R N T I J Y N N N F K I O I
Q S H O W U E E G A L Y J I H O A U P G
U M U B D A P S A C I D G A P D V Q H G
I A G U G J E W T T I R E A F B L P O O
L R S S N M C W T G O R W N X X B U P L
T G Y T I L L R D U U S C N I S S O P B
O A V O P N A H P Q K C Y L S Z L R V T
R T O U P M S A W C P T O E E C A G R C
N S V R O A S L O F I S F V A N S G O E
D N O W H D Q L G N U W A L T H L J A T
V I F K S R B J B E E U H Y P A W S Q M
```

BEE	GROUP QUILT	SEWING CIRCLE
BLOCK SWAP	GUILD	SHOP HOP
BLOGGING	INSTAGRAM	SHOPPING
BUS TOUR	MAGAZINE	SHOW
CLASS	MINI GROUP	SLICE QUILT
CRUISE	PINTEREST	SWAP
FABRIC COLLECTING	RETREAT	WORKSHOP

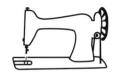

❊ Word RoundUp 7

BOUNTIFUL BASICS

```
M F H W C O M P L E M E N T A R Y W J R
E O R F O U N D A T I O N M T F M T A K
E E N E R F J C N Q R D E A J C O G F G
I R E O E G Y X Z R S R M T E G L J L G
I F G W C Z B Y D L E G L V U A Q O I G
K N U P K H E Q Q Q L Q M P N U V L T N
M Z A I I I R R E R U S A E M E P A T R
P M G N M T L O E X E W P C S N L K U M
G B G W O E N V M S K Q C X G C G L T N
E Z N H O L F C A Z G N A B F E J X P
L W I E O C D I T N T N D F P R M T V R
B C W E E T D R C T M I R E D A E R H T
M D E L G A G D N R J B C C O K R D X R
I R S N I W N U S O M X C O S R F A L K
H F O R T R H V X H F O D A G V C M T V
T L T Y E K I L J S N M B V S Z H A R S
```

☐ ☐ ☐ ☐ ☐ ☐ ☐   **7 helpful tools**

☐ ☐ ☐ ☐ ☐   **5 types of sleeves**

☐ ☐ ☐ ☐   **4 popular quilt block motifs**

☐ ☐ ☐   **3 color schemes**

☐ ☐   **2 quilt-related papers**

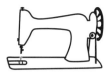

✖ Word RoundUp 8

SEWING SUITE

```
J  Q  A  T  W  C  O  R  R  L  B  K  W  M  L  U  R  M  F  F
U  T  N  M  X  R  R  V  T  D  K  I  V  G  W  E  A  R  R  A
H  O  A  J  J  U  E  A  E  M  Y  N  C  B  K  I  I  R  L  W
Y  A  U  U  J  C  T  S  Z  R  Q  T  E  P  R  E  O  B  O  F
E  U  S  J  P  R  F  E  H  Y  L  C  W  D  N  S  U  R  B  O
P  R  R  F  I  E  S  N  U  O  N  O  N  D  Q  M  K  X  O  B
A  M  I  S  H  H  T  T  S  E  W  N  C  Q  S  S  K  E  A  E
C  D  C  L  A  S  S  O  R  O  J  Z  S  K  H  V  T  S  U  L
S  W  K  P  P  B  B  E  S  B  P  O  L  O  C  D  T  Z  Q  B
D  Y  R  A  I  L  F  E  N  C  E  G  P  A  P  I  P  H  C  P
N  Q  V  Z  L  N  C  G  I  L  L  E  T  D  N  A  W  O  H  S
A  E  D  Q  O  E  N  Y  E  G  V  W  Y  G  S  D  I  F  M  T
L  Y  N  C  J  X  W  J  V  Y  E  K  H  Q  Q  B  M  V  Y  K
G  B  B  W  K  N  E  O  E  P  O  C  S  O  D  I  E  L  A  K
U  N  D  E  R  S  T  I  T  C  H  W  V  G  N  I  N  N  U  R
T  O  P  S  T  I  T  C  H  Z  N  I  A  H  C  H  S  I  R  I
```

☐ ☐ ☐ ☐ ☐ ☐ **6 quilt inspirations from others**

☐ ☐ ☐ ☐ ☐ **5 types of stitching**

☐ ☐ ☐ ☐ **4 quilt blocks**

☐ ☐ ☐ **3 quilt styles**

☐ ☐ **2 light colors**

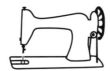

✳ Logic Puzzle 7

Intermediate

Lifetime Achievement Award

April Jacobs was the Lifetime Achievement honoree at the Heritage Quilter's annual show, where April displayed five of her award-winning quilts. Match each quilt to the year it was completed, the name of the quilt, the award it won, and the category it had been entered in.

1. The quilt completed in 2017 was entered in the Appliqué category.

2. *Darkness at Dawn* is either the miniature quilt or the quilt completed in 2016.

3. *Green Study* is not a wallhanging.

4. The art quilt was finished one year after the wallhanging.

5. *Darkness at Dawn* is not an art quilt.

6. *Green Study* was finished sometimes before the hand-quilted masterpiece.

7. The wallhanging was finished one year after the miniature quilt.

8. *Hopping Happy* is not hand quilted.

9. The quilt that won 1st place was finished three years before the 2nd place quilt.

10. Of the quilt that won Best in Show and the quilt finished in 2017, one is *Beige Is Beautiful* and the other is hand quilted.

11. The art quilt did not win Viewer's Choice.

		NAME					AWARD					CATEGORY				
		DARKNESS AT DAWN	GREEN STUDY	HOPPING HAPPY	FANCY STITCHES	BEIGE IS BEAUTIFUL	BEST IN SHOW	1ST PLACE	2ND PLACE	3RD PLACE	VIEWER'S CHOICE	MINIATURE	HAND QUILTING	APPLIQUÉ	ART QUILT	WALLHANGING
YEAR	2014															
	2015															
	2016															
	2017															
	2018															
CATEGORY	Miniature															
	Hand Quilting															
	Appliqué															
	Art Quilt															
	Wallhanging															
AWARD	Best in Show															
	1st Place															
	2nd Place															
	3rd Place															
	Viewer's Choice															

YEAR	NAME	AWARD	CATEGORY
2014			
2015			
2016			
2017			
2018			

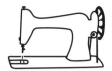

✦ Logic Puzzle 8

Intermediate > **Shop Hop**

Gabriel created his own "shop hop," planning a road trip to visit a new craft store each day. Figure out which craft store he visited each day, its specialty, as well as the town the store it was in.

1. The shop Gabriel visited on July 20 specializes in yarn.

2. Crafts & Things doesn't specialize in craft kits.

3. Gabriel visited Crafty Corner two days after he stopped in Bodega Bay.

4. The stop on July 22 wasn't in Bodega Bay.

5. The Craft Emporium visit was on July 20.

6. The five craft stores were the shop in Eureka, the stop on June 22, the shop specializing in craft kits, Crafty Corners, and the stop for quilter's cotton.

7. Crafts & Things was either in La Jolla or the shop with quilter's cotton.

8. The store in La Jolla, the stop on July 22, and Crafty Corner are three different shops.

9. Of the art materials store and the stop on July 22, one is in Pismo Beach and the other is Crafts R Us.

		CRAFT STORE					SPECIALTY					TOWN				
		Craft Emporium	Crafts R Us	Hometown Crafts	Crafty Corner	Crafts & Things	Yarn	Quilter's cotton	Home dec fabric	Craft kits	Art materials	Santa Cruz	Eureka	Bodega Bay	La Jolla	Pismo Beach
DAY	July 20															
	July 21															
	July 22															
	July 23															
	July 24															
TOWN	Santa Cruz															
	Eureka															
	Bodega Bay															
	La Jolla															
	Pismo Beach															
SPECIALTY	Yarn															
	Quilter's cotton															
	Home dec fabric															
	Craft kits															
	Art materials															

DAY	CRAFT STORE	SPECIALTY	TOWN
July 20			
July 21			
July 22			
July 23			
July 24			

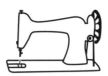

♥ Crossword Puzzle 8

PATTERN PARTS

ACROSS

3 big 4 search key

5 what to mark and cut

7 poetic prose

8 cutting counter cheat sheet

11 matching your skills

13 variations

14 instructional component

16 a matter of fit

17 from the front and side (e.g.)

18 personalization

DOWN

1 making the best use of materials (2 wds)

2 one of the Big 4

4 particularly helpful when on the cusp between two sizes (2 wds)

5 model

6 stitch placement (2 wds)

9 the little things that matter

10 fit guide (2 wds)

12 woven or stretch (e.g.)

15 selecting one dashed line or another (2 wds)

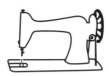

♥ Crossword Puzzle 9

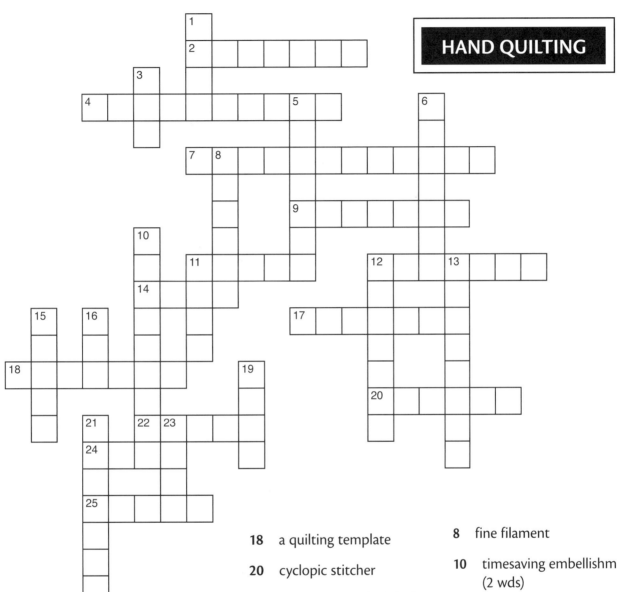

HAND QUILTING

ACROSS

2 every square inch

4 all one piece

7 unswerving mark

9 support or help

11 coffee, accent, dining (i.e)

12 also known as "tacking"

14 common city center layout

17 bird's coat

18 a quilting template

20 cyclopic stitcher

22 club, wing, or deck (i.e.)

24 repeat outline stitch

25 cutting device for stray threads

DOWN

1 can be Scotch or blue

3 opposite of bottom

5 mini shot delivery system

6 part of BFF

8 fine filament

10 timesaving embellishment (2 wds)

11 it flies

12 a lofty thing

13 style of earring

15 literary symbol

16 glass-head, flat, flower (i.e.)

19 leave one's ____

21 lotion for thread (2 wds)

23 an antebellum type of skirt

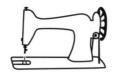

Word Search 9

Best in Show

```
R S E S S A L C U W N Z S P A W S I J C
P C D S N O B B I R J R L A N O I G E R
E A D P P K H S H O P P I N G I B U S Y
C A E X O Y H F R I E N D S G E S N H H
I G S J H L E C T U R E S L Q X P N S H
O N T U S S Q A E F D S Q I T H O A N Z
H I I D K E Z D N D E M S D B I N T T A
C P N G R I L O W V W A R E M B S I P D
S P A E O R N X O L K C O S R I O O S S
R I T D W T K L J Q P H D S A T R N E E
E H I M P N G T T A E I N Z G L X A Z C
W S O R P E D O H L V N E P N E T L I O
E X N U T L L A E R E E V Z O V S U R N
I O O I I L N B I H E I G N L A R Z P D
V R H U A D A A H I L E V A L R I Y N N
G W G B J L F E E S S R P H O T F L L B
```

BALLOT	FRIENDS	NATIONAL	SLIDES
BUS	GROUP	PRIZES	SPONSOR
CLASSES	GUILD	REGIONAL	SWAPS
DESTINATION	HAND	RIBBONS	TRAVEL
ENTRIES	JUDGED	SECOND	VENDORS
EXHIBIT	LABEL	SHIPPING	VIEWERS CHOICE
FAIR	LECTURES	SHOPPING	WHITE GLOVES
FEES	LONGARM	SLEEVE	WORKSHOP
FIRST	MACHINE		

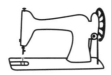

♠ Word Search 10

Sewing Machines

```
C M H O P P I N G F O O T C O R D E D C
A R T E P T S M G O U R H W R E G N I S
N N H B U H E E H G S I A N C G P S A D
M E R T E V X E A V X O N S A V I E T N
E M O T E R X Q F R V D D J M N Z A T I
T M A G E G N B H U S R C U S U L M A B
T B T F Y Y W I R Y E O R P T H A G C B
E L P E Z Y O Y N H W W A I K U J U H O
U A L E J I N Y T A K E N M O R E I M B
Y D A D L T O O F G N I K L A W X D E T
V E T D M E R E G Y L O N G A R M E N T
I P E O A B L N L M G T R E A D L E T Y
O T T G E D I D Y W O V E R L O C K S X
O O G S E K D T H G I E W R E H T A E F
L O L E I D H C T I T S T H G I A R T S
I F N V G I Q H E Y U P Y I J X D E T E
```

ATTACHMENTS	FEATHERWEIGHT	KENMORE	SINGER
BERNINA	FEED DOGS	LONGARM	STRAIGHT STITCH
BOBBIN	FEET	NEEDLE	THROAT PLATE
BROTHER	FOOT PEDAL	OIL	TREADLE
CAMS	HAND CRANK	OVERLOCK	VIKING
CANMETTE	HOPPING FOOT	SEAM GUIDE	WALKING FOOT
CORD	JUKI	SEARS	

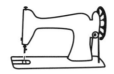

Word Scramble 7

Unscramble the words to find popular quilting terms.

CAID YDE _ _ _ _ _ _ _

IKATB _ _ _ _ _

OLRCO HWSA _ _ _ _ _ _ _ _ _

EDSRESIP _ _ _ _ _ _ _

MENMRIISO _ _ _ _ _ _ _ _

GIIDNO _ _ _ _ _ _

KIN _ _ _

OILOAKD _ _ _ _ _ _ _

SYO XAW _ _ _ _ _ _

ETSAM _ _ _ _ _

RALAUTN _ _ _ _ _ _ _

ORMBE _ _ _ _ _

DOAS HAS _ _ _ _ _ _ _

SHAIRA _ _ _ _ _ _

NPAGTNII _ _ _ _ _ _ _ _

PTNGEMI _ _ _ _ _ _ _

GVIENAR _ _ _ _ _ _ _

AREDDM _ _ _ _ _ _

VCAEERIT _ _ _ _ _ _ _ _

ITERSS _ _ _ _ _ _

RBEUBR DBNA _ _ _ _ _ _ _ _ _ _

SOIIRBH _ _ _ _ _ _ _

ATE _ _ _

ITE YDE _ _ _ _ _ _

RICNOOP _ _ _ _ _ _ _

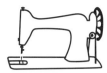

🧵 Word Scramble 8

Unscramble the words to find popular quilting terms.

FIBER AND NEEDLE ARTS

IATTNTG _ _ _ _ _ _ _

BEDNAGI _ _ _ _ _ _ _

EATPRYST _ _ _ _ _ _ _ _

LEDNEE ACLE _ _ _ _ _ _ _ _ _ _

THOERCC _ _ _ _ _ _ _

PIALUPEQ _ _ _ _ _ _ _ _

IFRCAB _ _ _ _ _ _

BIRFE _ _ _ _ _

NIKTIGNT _ _ _ _ _ _ _ _

OSRCS TITCHS _ _ _ _ _ _ _ _ _ _ _

OERIDEBYRM _ _ _ _ _ _ _ _ _ _

CUETL _ _ _ _ _

XDIME DIEAM _ _ _ _ _ _ _ _ _ _

NPENTEEOIDL _ _ _ _ _ _ _ _ _ _ _

NUTGILIQ _ _ _ _ _ _ _ _

NGIVEAW _ _ _ _ _ _ _

Criss Cross 7

13 letters

MINI CHARM PACK

ROLLIE POLLIES

11 letters

CHARM SQUARE

SKINNY STRIP

10 letters

FAT QUARTER

PIXIE STRIP

9 letters

CHARM ROLL

FAT EIGHTH

HONEY BUN

JELLY ROLL

LAYER CAKE

PATTY CAKE

8 letters

HALF YARD

FLAT FOLD

SELVEDGE

TURNOVER

7 letters

BALIPOP

STACKER

6 letters

HEXIES

5 letters

STRIP

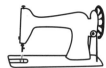

QUILT BLOCKS

Criss Cross 8

15 letters

DUTCHMANS
PUZZLE

12 letters

CORN AND
BEANS

BROKEN DISHES

11 letters

GOOSE TRACKS

FOOLS PUZZLE

SNAILS TRAIL

10 letters

CROSSROADS

IRISH CHAIN

9 letters

APPLE CORE

CARD TRICK

CHURN DASH

DAIRY BARN

FOUR PATCH

HOURGLASS

MAPLE LEAF

NINE PATCH

PINWHEEL

8 letters

LOG CABIN

SNOWBALL

7 letters

BEAR PAW

CHEVRON

DIAMOND

DRESDEN

HEXAGON

SHOOFLY

6 letters

BASKET

BOW TIE

SPOOLS

5 letters

HOUSE

3 letters

LILY

TREE

YOYO

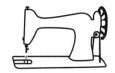

Word RoundUp 9

QUILTING QUIRKS

```
Z H J P C O V R S H O W A N D T E L L E
B H F L H H F M V L F Q G J B T N I O P
H O C A D O J L X L S E S S A L C U H F
O X O U Z R T M E S C F E Y E S G B L B
B B G K I Z V O H H W T O R J L K O X G
H W S Z G D V A G M N G L A O B S N R B
K S E C F P F E A R P R N D H S O A B G
N E X F A T S G H G A I O I Y T I S R J
R G J Z F R A I V E C P J O T N F U E D
E D N E K Z F L P F W P H O L E Z T K I
J E T R I U E J Q E F W C L E F E D Z I
I V N N E V A R R W V E R D U M E M N V
W L E X O T K U X R L Y A Z E T B L Q U
R E F O E D T C T R T T Y X T M M P I M
F S R Z Y A L A E B O L T B T B I A S T
E G Y G N T G P P N G N E Q C I R B A F
```

□ □ □ □ □ □ □   **7 personal quilt inspirations**

□ □ □ □ □   **5 parts of a needle**

□ □ □ □   **4 material terms**

□ □ □   **3 guild activities**

□ □   **2 embroidery threads**

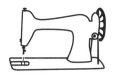

✕ Word RoundUp 10

DESIGN DECISIONS

```
P  I  L  L  O  W  Q  T  E  R  N  H  V  F  K  T  H  G  I  L
G  K  C  B  J  P  N  F  A  B  S  X  Q  S  K  C  A  F  W  V
J  O  U  U  N  V  W  E  K  B  X  Q  Y  Y  W  N  H  A  A  S
Z  F  F  Y  R  M  E  N  E  P  L  Z  N  T  E  Q  D  L  L  H
K  A  O  B  C  T  I  G  R  D  D  E  E  U  V  U  A  I  I  R
E  V  X  I  O  T  A  G  O  A  U  L  C  Y  N  N  P  V  F  Y
R  R  G  A  L  Z  D  I  E  G  E  Y  D  L  C  C  P  U  S  P
E  Q  D  Y  O  A  L  R  N  Y  N  E  N  E  O  D  B  P  F  H
P  G  H  T  R  A  P  O  E  B  A  C  N  V  Y  T  O  P  T  L
A  F  A  C  E  S  C  L  Z  O  J  E  E  Y  P  P  N  H  N  H
P  L  L  I  D  Z  H  Y  H  Z  G  R  G  G  C  I  R  B  A  F
H  I  M  E  P  G  D  U  R  A  T  O  N  K  H  C  N  E  R  F
P  C  B  O  E  Y  G  I  R  W  I  H  M  E  N  I  H  C  A  M
A  N  I  V  N  U  A  O  T  Y  N  Z  M  P  E  J  Y  Z  X  E
R  E  S  K  S  H  T  I  S  L  E  N  N  A  L  F  D  X  K  T
G  P  D  L  C  S  F  F  Y  A  R  B  M  A  H  C  J  X  B  S
```

☐ ☐ ☐ ☐ ☐ ☐ **6 home decor items to sew**

☐ ☐ ☐ ☐ ☐ **5 sewing space must-haves**

☐ ☐ ☐ ☐ **4 fabric types**

☐ ☐ ☐ **3 design tools**

☐ ☐ **2 embroidery stitches**

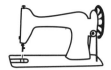

✸ Logic Puzzle 9

Modern Miniatures

The West Bay Modern Quilters held a year-long guild challenge in which members competed to make the most miniature quilts. Five close friends decided to challenge themselves further by choosing a color theme within which she or he would work. Match all the quilters with the number of quilts they completed, the color theme they chose, and the size of miniature they preferred.

1. Todd didn't make 8 quilts.

2. Neither the person who used complementary colors nor Sophie was the quilter who favored 5″ × 8″ quilts.

3. Of the person who liked 5″ × 6″ quilts and the quilter who made 5″ × 8″ quilts, one was Kerry and the other made 10 quilts.

4. The quilter who used warm tones made one more quilt than the quilter who stuck to black-and-white fabrics.

5. The quilter whose quilts were 10″ × 10″ made one fewer quilt than the person who made 5″ × 8″ quilts.

6. Sophie didn't use warm tones.

7. Greg didn't make 4″ × 5″ quilts.

8. The quilter who made 5″ × 6″ quilts worked in black-and-white.

9. Greg made 12 quilts.

10. Of the quilter who made 10″ × 10″ quilts and Greg, one quilter made 8 quilts and the other's quilts were monochromatic.

		QUILTER					THEME					SIZE				
		Kerry	Greg	Sophie	Todd	Sue	Complementary colors	Warm tones	Black-and-white	Triadic colors	Monochromatic	4″ × 5″	5″ × 6″	5″ × 8″	7″ × 9″	10″ × 10″
QUILT	8															
	9															
	10															
	11															
	12															
SIZE	4″ × 5″															
	5″ × 6″															
	5″ × 8″															
	7″ × 9″															
	10″ × 10″															
THEME	Complementary colors															
	Warm tones															
	Black-and-white															
	Triadic colors															
	Monochromatic															

QUILT	QUILTER	THEME	SIZE
8			
9			
10			
11			
12			

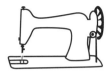

✦ Logic Puzzle 10

Show-and-Tell

Five friends are attending a quilt retreat. On Show-and-Tell Night, each of the friends plans to share their favorite quilts. Match the quilters with their hometowns, the order in which they will present, and the number of quilts they brought to share.

1. Of the quilter who brought 4 quilts and the one going 5th, one is from Oakland and the other is Tony.

2. Kennedy will show 8 quilts.

3. Jake is either the quilter who will share 8 quilts or the one presenting 3rd.

4. Estefany is showing one quilt more than her friend presenting 2nd.

5. Of the quilters going 5th and 4th, one is from Orinda and one is Tony.

6. Eric, the quilter from San Leandro, and the person presenting 5th are three different people.

7. The person who brought 5 quilts is either the person going 4th or the quilter from Berkeley.

8. The quilter from Concord brought one fewer quilt than the quilter going 5th.

		QUILTER					HOMETOWN					PRESENTATION ORDER				
		Tony	Kennedy	Jake	Eric	Estefany	Oakland	Concord	Berkeley	Orinda	San Leandro	1st	2nd	3rd	4th	5th
QUILT TO PRESENT	4															
	5															
	6															
	7															
	8															
PRESENTATION ORDER	1st															
	2nd															
	3rd															
	4th															
	5th															
HOMETOWN	Oakland															
	Concord															
	Berkeley															
	Orinda															
	San Leandro															

QUILT	QUILTER	HOMETOWN	ORDER
4			
5			
6			
7			
8			

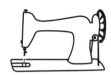

♥ Crossword Puzzle 10

COLORS OF LIFE

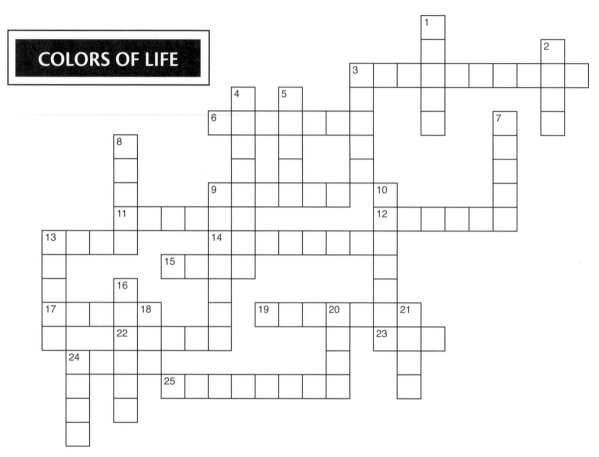

ACROSS

3 creeping myrtle

6 pink flowering shrub

9 reddish pink

11 a plant of the genus *Viola*

12 grape-colored

13 citrus fruit

14 flowery scent or flavor

15 blue green

17 you might find a very old mosquito in it

19 deep red

22 citrus fruit

23 lay out in the sun

24 precious metal

25 12:00 a.m.

DOWN

1 building material

2 sad

3 famous Georgia export

4 bronze formerly used for making cannons

5 popular pants style

7 earthy pigment

8 fruit used to make oil

9 jade green

10 fruit related to peaches and plums

13 blooming deciduous shrub

16 part of CMYK

18 lobster colored

20 variety of herbal tea

21 branch of U.S. Armed Forces

24 mix of black and white

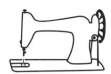

♥ Crossword Puzzle 11

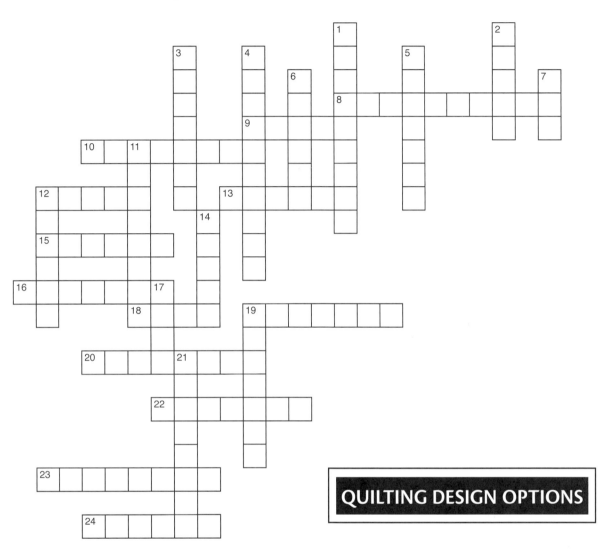

QUILTING DESIGN OPTIONS

ACROSS

8   key component of crazy quilting

9   make your mark or for posterity

10   needle-turn, fusible (i.e.)

12   acrylic, oil, water (i.e.)

13   Churn Dash, Log Cabin, Bear Paw (i.e.)

15   made with patchwork

16   not laid out straight (2 wds)

18   large, medium, or small (i.e.)

19   quilt top layout

20   pieces of quartz

22   wadding

23   Part of FMQ

24   wing it

DOWN

1   embroider

2   everything in its place

3   the finishing touch

4   all one piece

5   on the outside or along the edge

6   woven or stretch (e.g.)

7   colorer or stain

11   Simplicity product

12   decorative element in cakes, quilts

14   what Justice holds in her hand

17   sometimes done with yarn

19   something comes between us

21   this block requires stuffing

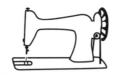

✦ Word Search 11

Retreats

```
Y F L C B M Z K F Y D L S E I L P P U S
A A E C A B E X C R J A E T A M M O O R
B B C D H R M A P A I C R L B U N E P W
W R T W I O T S L I O E B X G V N U O D
R I U H J A C X L S I C N S N L S R V P
U C R K B C L O Q K N R B D S X K Q C C
R J E U B L O H L I O O E E S S S Y Z P
G Z W O B S L Y A A I T W R H E A D J S
K D N O S S E L A F T P C O W Q U L N X
F O F C Z W W B U U A E P I Y B B Q C F
U O Z Q V M O T N N N J N L H V K D N J
Q F M W Y P N H I L I G O G N I G D O L
W I T F F X Q I S P T C F F A R E M A C
X M W S N A C K S W S A R E T H G U A L
P L A N E L Z Z U O E B O U D F V L B K
Z S C H E D U L E E D A Z E N I H C A M
```

CAMERA	FUN	ROOMMATE
CAR	LAUGHTER	SCHEDULE
CHOCOLATE	LECTURE	SEWING
CLASS	LESSON	SHOW
DESTINATION	LODGING	SNACKS
FABRIC	MACHINE	SUPPLIES
FOOD	MEALS	WORKSHOP
FRIENDS	PLANE	

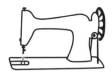

♦ Word Search 12

Sewing Machine Feet

```
C Z F R S F O N Q O J R O L L E R G Z J
F I P R W N H U G U P Z S C A A Z E J G
W P A I I X K O Q T A E H A W O R R A N
G P P D H N T A D H S R N O L Z O T N L
Z E P N W E G T H N Y A T T M Y H G G A
O R L S N J C E U N E I C E O E V K P J
V N I L D L H N O I T N M R R E K G L Z
Z T Q O A P K Y M F O O G I E I U T J A
Y E U C C J O I N I N G N E V N O Y G
W P E A R F R A T Y H G G I U O C R A
L A Z K E H H O V R J T M N N D P Z H Z
I T Z Z S L M C O R D I N G I I T P G
C S L K S E H O V E R L O C K K N A X I
C A L Z E E L O H N O T T U B T L R R Z
I I H R R B L I N D H E M J X P P A A B
T B F G P A J Z B C Q C V A A K H B W D
```

APPLIQUÉ	FRINGE	PRESSER
BIAS TAPE	GATHERING	QUARTER-INCH
BLIND HEM	JOINING	ROLLER
BRAIDING	LACE	WALKING
BUTTONHOLE	NARROW	ZIGZAG
CORDING	OPEN-TOE	ZIPPER
DARNING	OVERCAST	
FREE-MOTION	OVERLOCK	

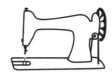

❧ Word Mine 7

See how many words you can make out of the letters in popular needle styles!

PINS & NEEDLES

MILLINER

7-letter words (2)

— — — — — — —

— — — — — — —

6-letter words (7)

— — — — — —

— — — — — —

— — — — — —

— — — — — —

— — — — — —

— — — — — —

5-letter words (9)

— — — — —

— — — — —

— — — — —

— — — — —

— — — — —

— — — — —

— — — — —

— — — — —

— — — — —

4-letter words (23)

— — — —

— — — —

— — — —

— — — —

— — — —

— — — —

— — — —

— — — —

— — — —

— — — —

— — — —

— — — —

— — — —

— — — —

— — — —

— — — —

— — — —

— — — —

— — — —

— — — —

— — — —

— — — —

— — — —

3-letter words (18)

— — —

— — —

— — —

— — —

— — —

— — —

— — —

— — —

— — —

— — —

— — —

— — —

— — —

— — —

— — —

2-letter words (10)

— —

— —

— —

— —

— —

— —

— —

Solutions

✴ Logic Puzzle Sample—JUNE BUG QUILT MEETING

ORDER	QUILTER	PROJECT
1	Kerry	Anniversary quilt
2	Sue	Wallhanging
3	Betsy	Patchwork pillow
4	Alice	Baby quilt

♥ Crossword Puzzle 1—GARMENT TERMS

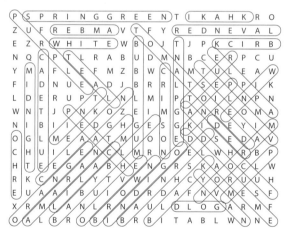

Word Scramble 1—MACHINE STITCHES

BAR TACK	FINISHING	SCALLOP
BASTING	COUCHING	OVERCAST
TACKING	GATHERING	LADDER
BLIND HEM	SATIN	OVERLOCK
STRAIGHT	ROLLED EDGE	DECORATIVE
STRETCH	EDGE	HONEYCOMB
ZIGZAG	DOUBLE NEEDLE	SHELL TUCK
BUTTONHOLE	COVERSTITCH	

Word Scramble 2—QUILTING TERMS

STIPPLE	HAND	STITCH
ALLOVER	FEATHER	TIE
BACKSTITCH	FREE-MOTION	TRAPUNTO
HOOP	MEANDER	WHOLECLOTH
BEESWAX	PANTOGRAPH	GRID
CROSSHATCH	GLOVES	STENCIL
DESIGN	BATTING	BASTING
ECHO	THREAD	TENSION

▲ Word Search 1—COLOR PLAY

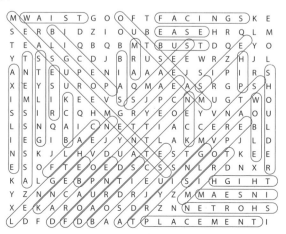

Criss Cross 1—MATERIAL TERMS

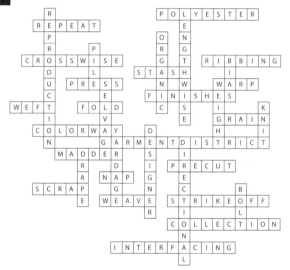

▲ Word Search 2—IT'S A MATTER OF FIT

Criss Cross 2—FABRIC TYPES

73

Word RoundUp 1—SEWING SELECTIONS

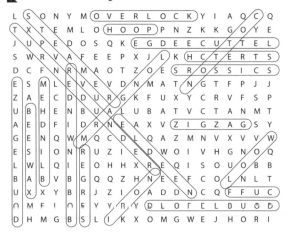

Word RoundUp 2—PROJECT PERFECTION

Logic Puzzle 1—SWEATSHIRT SHOPPING

SIZE	BUYER	COLOR
Small	Melissa	Purple
Medium	Toni	Green
Large	Bridget	Red
Extra-large	Jane	Blue

Logic Puzzle 2—QUILT GROUP CHALLENGE

PIECES	PATTERN	QUILTER
1,310	Log Cabin	Kris
1,440	Nine Patch	Jan
1,570	Winding Ways	Dina
1,700	Jacob's Ladder	Stacy

Word Mine 1—DENIM

5-LETTER WORD (1)

MINED

4-LETTER WORDS (9)

DENI
DIME
DINE
IDEM
MEND

MIEN
MIND
MINE
NIDE

3-LETTER WORDS (9)

DEN
DIE
DIM

DIN
END
MED
MEN
MID
NIM

ED
EM
EN
ID
IN
ME

MI

2-LETTER WORDS (9)

NE

DE

Word Mine 2—BETWEEN

5-LETTER WORDS (2)

ETWEE
TWEEN

4-LETTER WORDS (12)

BEEN
BEET
BENE
BENT

EEEW
NEWB
NEWT
TEEN
TWEE
WEEN
WEET
WENT

3-LETTER WORDS (16)

BEE
BEN
BET
EEW
EWE
NEB

NEE
NET
NEW
TEE
TEN
TEW
WEB
WEE
WEN

WET

2-LETTER WORDS (7)

BE
EN
ET
EW
NE
TE
WE

Crossword Puzzle 2—GARMENT PARTS

Crossword Puzzle 3—GENERAL SEWING

Word Search 3—QUILTING TECHNIQUES

◤ Word Search 4 — SEWING MACHINE PARTS

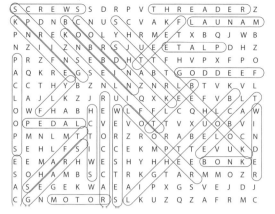

Word Scramble 3 — STITCHERY

THIMBLE
BLOCKING
STITCH
COUCHING
COUNTED

CROSSHATCHING
DARN
EMBROIDERY
EVENWEAVE
EYE

FLOSS
HOOP
CHATELAINE
CANDLEWICKING
NEEDLES

NEEDLEWORK
PERLE COTTON
REDWORK
SAMPLER
SEW
THREAD

Word Scramble 4 — ART QUILTING

BEADING
DIMENSIONAL
EMBELLISHING
DEPTH
MIXED MEDIA
SURFACE DESIGN

PAINT
THREAD SKETCHING
COLLAGE
LAYERING
DYEING

FABRIC FOLDING
IMPROVISATION
INK
LANDSCAPE
PHOTO TRANSFER
SHIBORI

◣ Criss Cross 3 — QUILT PARTS

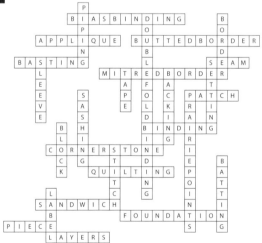

◣ Criss Cross 4 — ACTIONS USED IN QUILTING

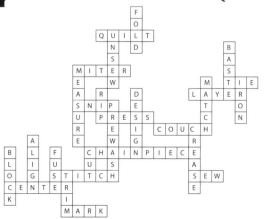

◥ Word RoundUp 3 — SEWING SUPERSTARS

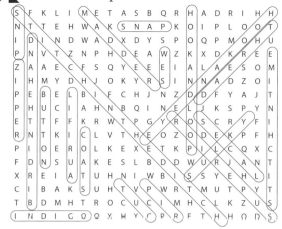

◤ Word RoundUp 4 — PIECING PROFESSION

▦ Logic Puzzle 3 — QUILTING QUERIES

TIME	QUILTER	CHALLENGE
10 a.m.	Tim	Bindings
11 a.m.	Linda	Curved piecing
12 noon	Sarah	Batting
1 p.m.	Alice	Corners

▦ Logic Puzzle 4 — TRYING NEW PROJECTS

MONTH	SEWIST	PROJECT	PATTERN
January	Betsy	Shorts	Paisley
February	Jennifer	Place mats	Floral
March	Zinnia	Bike basket	Gingham
April	Amber	Tunic	Plaid

◣ Word Mine 3 — CREWEL

5-LETTER WORD (1)
CREEL

4-LETTER WORDS (9)
CERE
CLEW
CREW
EWER
LEER
REEL
WEEL

WEER
WERE

3-LETTER WORDS (10)
CEE
CEL
EEL
EEW
ERE
EWE
LEE

REC
REE
WEE

2-LETTER WORDS (5)
EL
ER
EW
RE
WE

Word Mine 4 — SHARP

5-LETTER WORD (1)	3-LETTER WORDS (15)		2-LETTER WORDS (6)
HARPS	PARS	PAR	RAH
4-LETTER WORDS (9)	PASH	PAS	AH
HAPS	RAPS	RAH	AR
HARP	RASH	RAP	AS
HASP	RASP	RAS	HA
	SPAR	SAP	PA
	AHS	SHA	SH
	ARS	SPA	
	ASH		
	ASP		
	HAP		
	HAS		
	PAH		

Crossword Puzzle 4 — WHAT CAN YOU SEW?

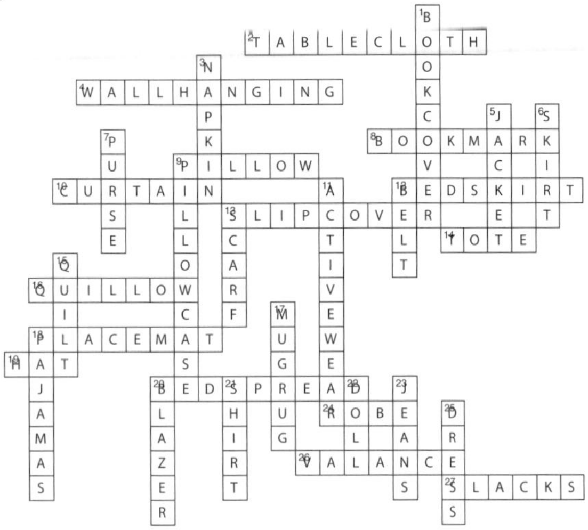

(crossword grid with answers: TABLECLOTH, WALLHANGING, BOOKMARK, PILLOW, CURTAIN, SLIPCOVER, BEDSKIRT, TOTE, QUILLOW, PLACEMAT, HAT, BEDSPREAD, ROBE, VALANCE, SLACKS, etc.)

Crossword Puzzle 5 — PINS AND NEEDLES

(crossword grid with answers: LEATHER, UPHOLSTERY, SHARPS, SCARF, HEAD, TAPESTRY, DARN, CREWELS, FLOWERHEAD, EYE, BAND, MILLINER, BLUNTTIP, etc.)

Word Search 5 — DESIGN TOOLS

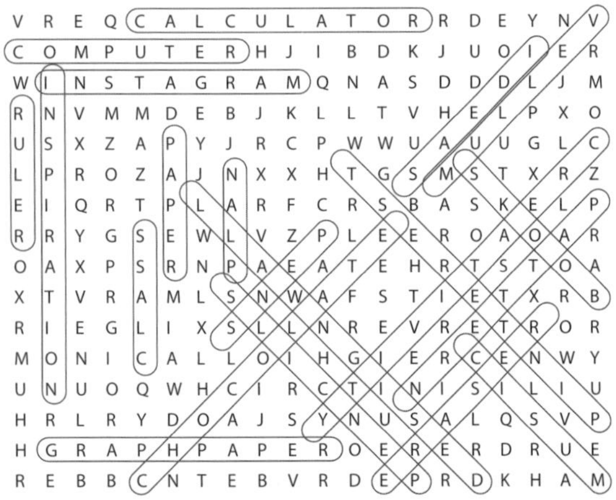

V	R	E	Q	C	A	L	C	U	L	A	T	O	R	R	D	E	Y	N	V
C	O	M	P	U	T	E	R	H	J	I	B	D	K	J	U	O	I	E	R
W	I	N	S	T	A	G	R	A	M	Q	N	A	S	D	D	D	L	J	M
R	N	V	M	M	D	E	B	J	K	L	L	T	V	H	E	L	P	X	O
U	S	X	Z	A	P	Y	J	R	C	P	W	W	U	A	U	U	G	L	C
L	P	R	O	Z	A	J	N	X	X	H	T	S	M	S	T	X	R	Z	Z
E	I	R	Y	G	S	E	W	L	V	Z	P	E	E	R	O	A	O	A	R
R	R	O	A	X	P	S	R	N	P	A	E	A	T	E	H	R	T	S	T
O	A	X	P	S	R	N	P	A	E	A	T	E	H	R	T	S	T	O	A
X	T	V	R	A	M	L	S	X	N	W	A	F	S	T	I	E	T	X	R
R	I	E	G	L	I	L	X	S	N	R	E	V	R	E	T	R	O	R
M	O	N	I	C	A	L	L	O	I	H	G	I	E	R	C	E	N	W	Y
U	N	U	O	Q	W	H	C	I	R	C	T	I	N	I	S	I	L	L	U
H	R	L	R	Y	D	O	A	J	S	Y	N	U	S	A	L	Q	S	V	P
H	G	R	A	P	H	P	A	P	E	R	O	E	R	E	R	D	R	U	E
R	E	B	B	C	N	T	E	B	V	R	D	E	P	R	D	K	H	A	M

Word Search 6 — INTERFACING

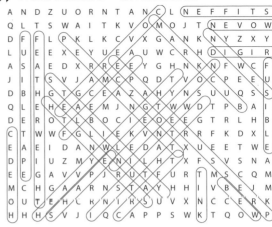

A	N	D	Z	U	O	R	N	T	A	N	C	L	N	E	F	F	I	T	S		
Q	L	T	S	W	A	I	T	K	V	O	M	O	J	T	N	E	V	O	W		
D	F	F	L	P	K	L	K	C	V	X	G	A	N	K	N	Y	Z	X	Y		
L	U	E	E	X	E	Y	U	E	A	U	W	C	R	H	D	I	G	I	R		
A	S	A	E	D	X	R	R	E	E	Y	G	H	K	N	F	W	C	F		
J	I	T	H	G	T	G	C	E	A	Z	A	H	Y	N	S	U	U	Q	S		
D	B	H	E	A	E	H	X	Z	W	V	W	D	T	P	B	A	I			
Q	L	E	R	O	T	L	B	O	C	I	E	O	E	E	G	T	R	L	H		
D	E	R	O	T	L	B	O	C	I	E	O	E	E	G	T	R	L	H			
C	T	W	W	F	G	L	I	E	K	V	N	T	R	R	F	K	D	X	L		
E	A	E	I	D	A	N	W	L	E	D	A	T	X	U	E	E	T	W	E		
E	P	I	U	Z	M	Y	E	N	L	H	T	X	F	S	V	S	N	A			
D	E	G	A	V	V	P	J	R	U	T	F	U	R	T	M	S	C	Q	M		
M	C	H	G	A	A	R	N	S	T	A	Y	H	H	I	V	B	E	J	M		
O	U	T	E	H	L	K	N	I	R	S	U	V	X	N	C	C	E	R	K		
H	H	H	S	V	J	I	Q	C	A	P	P	S	W	K	T	Q	O	W	P		

Word Scramble 5 — CLEANED AND PRESSED

IRON	HANG OUT	LOAD
STEAM	PERMANENT PRESS	WASH
PRESS CLOTH	LAUNDER	BLEACH
SEAM ROLL	BLEED	HANG
HAM	RUN	HAND WASH
SLEEVE BOARD	DRIP DRY	DELICATE
SOLE PLATE	LAUNDER	CARE
	SPIN	FINISH

Word Scramble 6 — Color Wheel

ANALOGOUS	DYE	WARM
COLOR THEORY	GRAY SCALE	SATURATION
TINT	HUE	PRIMARY
VALUE	SHADE	SECONDARY
COLOR WHEEL	BLENDING	TERTIARY
COMPLEMENTARY	TRIADIC	TONE
COOL	VALUE FINDER	SPECTRUM

Criss Cross 5 — QUILT STYLES

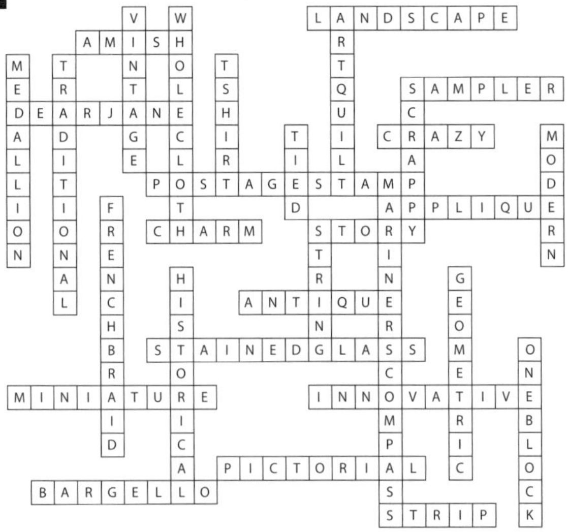

(criss cross grid with answers: AMISH, LANDSCAPE, SAMPLER, DEARJANE, CRAZY, POSTAGESTAMP, APPLIQUE, CHARM, STORY, ANTIQUE, STAINEDGLASS, MINIATURE, INNOVATIVE, PICTORIAL, BARGELLO, STRIP, etc.)

Criss Cross 6 — QUILTING TOOLS

Word RoundUp 5 — PLAYING WITH NOTIONS

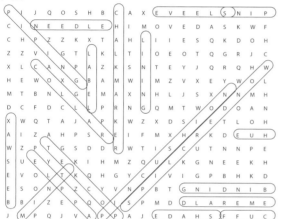

Word RoundUp 6 — FABRIC FUN

Logic Puzzle 5 — FLOWER EMBROIDERY

PRICE	EMBROIDERER	FLOWER	PROJECT
$3	Amy	Iris	Cuff bracelet
$5	Lynn	Rose	Gift tags
$7	Dawn	Violet	Sachet
$9	Jessica	Peony	Wall art

Logic Puzzle 6 — ROAD TRIPS!

YEAR	FRIEND	THEME	STATE
2016	Roxane	Rainbow	Indiana
2017	Debbie	Appliqué	Ohio
2018	Tristan	Traditional	Illinois
2019	Liz	Stash busting	Kentucky

Word Mine 5 — STRETCH

6-LETTER WORD (1)

CHERTS

5-LETTER WORDS (8)

CERTS
CHERT
CHEST
CREST
RETCH
TECHS
TETHS
TRETS

4-LETTER WORDS (21)

CERT
ECHT
ERST
ETCH
ETHS
HERS
HEST
HETS
RECS
RESH
REST
RETS
SECT
SETT
STET
TECH
TECS
TEST
TETH
TETS
TRET

3-LETTER WORDS (17)

ERS
EST
ETH
HER
HES
HET
REC
RES
RET
SEC
SER
SET
SHE
TEC
TES
TET
THE

2-LETTER WORDS (8)

EH
ER
ES
ET
HE
RE
SH
TE

Word Mine 6 — DARNER

6-LETTER WORD (1)

ERRAND

5-LETTER WORDS (6)

DARER
DENAR
DREAR
RARED
REDAN
RERAN

4-LETTER WORDS (13)

DARE
DARN
DEAN
DEAR
EARN
NARD

NEAR
NERD
RAND
RARE
READ
REAR
REND

3-LETTER WORDS (14)

AND
ANE
ARE
DAN
DEN
EAR
END
ERA
ERN

ERR
NAE
RAD
RAN
RED

2-LETTER WORDS (12)

AD
AE
AN
AR
DA
DE
ED
EN
ER
NA
NE
RE

Crossword Puzzle 6 — FOUND IN A SEWING SPACE

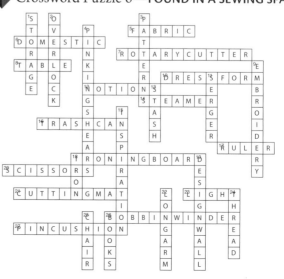

Crossword Puzzle 7—FABRIC PATTERNS

Word RoundUp 8—SEWING SUITE

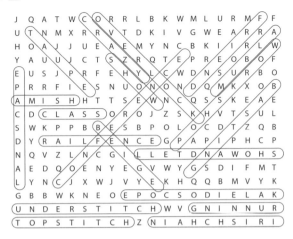

Word Search 7—GENERAL SEWING

Word Search 8—QUILTER'S ACTIVITIES

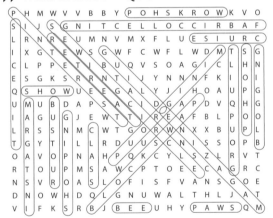

Word RoundUp 7—BOUNTIFUL BASICS

Logic Puzzle 7—LIFETIME ACHIEVEMENT AWARD

YEAR	NAME	AWARD	CATEGORY
2014	*Darkness at Dawn*	1st Place	Miniature
2015	*Hopping Happy*	Viewer's Choice	Wallhanging
2016	*Green Study*	3rd Place	Art Quilt
2017	*Beige Is Beautiful*	2nd Place	Appliqué
2018	*Fancy Stitches*	Best in Show	Hand Quilting

Logic Puzzle 8—SHOP HOP

DAY	CRAFT STORE	SPECIALTY	TOWN
July 20	Craft Emporium	Yarn	Eureka
July 21	Crafts & Things	Quilter's cotton	Bodega Bay
July 22	Crafts R Us	Home dec fabric	Santa Cruz
July 23	Crafty Corner	Art materials	Pismo Beach
July 24	Hometown Crafts	Craft kits	La Jolla

Crossword Puzzle 8—PATTERN PARTS

♥ Crossword Puzzle 9—HAND QUILTING

📖 Word Scramble 8—FIBER AND NEEDLE ARTS

TATTING	FABRIC	LUCET
BEADING	FIBER	MIXED MEDIA
TAPESTRY	KNITTING	NEEDLEPOINT
NEEDLE LACE	CROSS-STITCH	QUILTING
CROCHET	EMBROIDERY	WEAVING
APPLIQUÉ		

◤ Criss Cross 7—FABRIC PRECUTS

◤ Criss Cross 8—QUILT BLOCKS

✿ Word Search 9—BEST IN SHOW

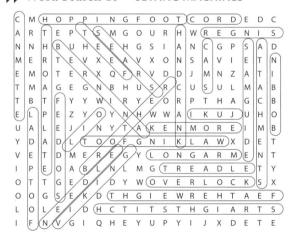

✿ Word Search 10—SEWING MACHINES

✖ Word RoundUp 9—QUILTING QUIRKS

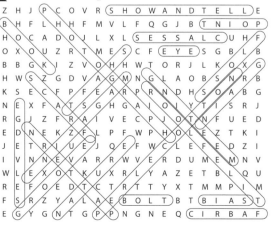

📖 Word Scramble 7—DYEING

ACID DYE	KOOLAID	PAINTING	SHIBORI
BATIK	SOY WAX	PIGMENT	TEA
COLOR WASH	STEAM	VINEGAR	TIE-DYE
DISPERSE	NATURAL	MADDER	PROCION
IMMERSION	OMBRÉ	REACTIVE	
INDIGO	SODA ASH	RESIST	
INK	ARASHI	RUBBER BAND	

Word RoundUp 10—DESIGN DECISIONS

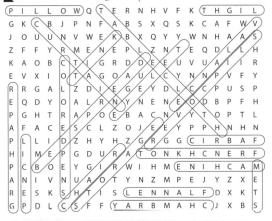

Crossword Puzzle 11—QUILTING DESIGN OPTIONS

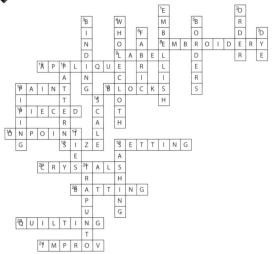

Logic Puzzle 9—MODERN MINIATURES

QUILT	QUILTER	THEME	SIZE
8	Sue	Complementary	10″ × 10″
9	Kerry	Triadic	5″ × 8″
10	Sophie	Black-and-white	5″ × 6″
11	Todd	Warm tones	4″ × 5″
12	Greg	Monochromatic	7″ × 9″

Logic Puzzle 10—SHOW-AND-TELL

QUILT	QUILTER	HOMETOWN	ORDER
4	Eric	Oakland	2nd
5	Estefany	Orinda	4th
6	Jake	Concord	3rd
7	Tony	Berkeley	5th
8	Kennedy	San Leandro	1st

Word Search 11—RETREATS

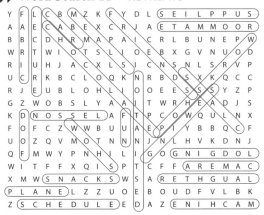

Crossword Puzzle 10—COLORS OF LIFE

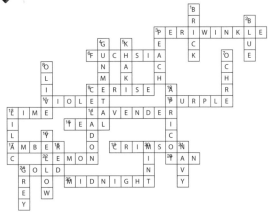

Word Search 12—SEWING MACHINE FEET

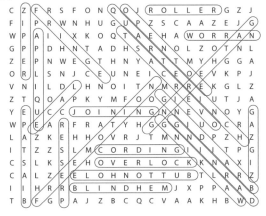

Word Mine 7—MILLINER

7-LETTER WORDS (2)

MILLIER
MILLINE

6-LETTER WORDS (7)

INLIER
LIMIER
LIMNER
LINIER
MERLIN
MILLER
NIELLI

5-LETTER WORDS (9)

ILLER
IMINE
LIMEN
LINER
MILER
MILLE
MINER
MIRIN
RILLE

4-LETTER WORDS (23)

EMIR
LIEN
LIER
LIME
LIMN
LINE
LIRE
LIRI
MELL
MERL
MIEN
MILE
MILL
MINE
MINI
MIRE
MIRI
NILL
REIN
RIEL
RILE
RILL
RIME

3-LETTER WORDS (18)

ELL
ELM
ERN
ILL
IRE
LEI
LIE
LIN
MEL
MEN
MIL
MIR
NIL
NIM
REI
REM
RIM
RIN

2-LETTER WORDS (10)

EL
EM
EN
ER
IN
LI
ME
MI
NE
RE